Never Come Back

∿

Never Come Back

A Cambodian Woman's Journey

∾

BY

Darina Siv

THE WRITER PRESS / ST. PAUL, MINNESOTA

The Writer Press
P.O. Box 16354
Saint Paul, MN 55116

ISBN 0-9702428-0-8

ACKNOWLEDGMENTS

Thanks to the Leadership Initiative Neighborhood Program
through the The Saint Paul Companies,
which made this book possible as part of my healing.

To my beloved parents

—————— First trip to Thailand, April 1979
—·—·—·—·— Second trip to Refugee Camp, December 1979

Cambodian Words Used in This Book

Angkar — the Khmer Rouge organization

Ka-Nak-Sa-Hak-Kaor — commune chief

Kramar — a long scarf that Khmer farmers use to cover their head to protect them from the sun.

Mekang — a group leader

Phoum — village

Sa-Hakaor — commune

Srok — district

Tamban — region

Yothea — a Communist Khmer Rouge soldier

Darina Siv and Family

Grandmother — — — — — — — — — Grandfather

Huoth Horn		Ty Nguon
	1- Daughter	Ty Chan Heang (deceased)
	2- Son	Ty Cheang Han (deceased)
	3- Daughter	Ty Chan Heng
	4- Daughter	Ty Cheang Ny
	5- Son	Ty Kim Toc
	6- Son	Ty Kim Tav (deceased)

Mother: Ty Chan Heang — — — — — Father: Cheng Siv

1- Daughter	Darina Siv (Rina)
2- Son	Darinal Siv (Nal)
3- Daughter	Dasina Siv (Mouch)
4- Son	Darino Siv (No)
5- Son	Chhinara Siv (Nara)
6- Daughter	Sokna Siv
7-Son	Chhinaro Siv
8- Daughter	Soknaroeun Siv
9- Son	Chhinaroth Siv

My third trip to Cambodia in 1998. After searching a long time,
I found the place where I buried my father in 1976.

Return to Cambodia

IN DECEMBER 1991, I made the difficult decision to visit my family in Cambodia the following spring. I have to face it, I told myself, it has haunted me for so long. I had not been back to my homeland since June 1979, when I escaped the hell of the Khmer Rouge regime and fled to Thailand and eventually to the United States, where I have lived ever since.

I left for Cambodia on May 21, 1992. My daughter, Nancy, had just turned four and my son, George, was twenty-one months old. With mixed feelings, I hugged my children and my husband, Terry, before boarding the Northwest Airlines jet. I was looking forward to spending time with friends and family, to eating the foods I liked and seeing the trees and land I missed. But I was also afraid.

I stayed overnight in Phnom Penh before going to my home village, Kompong Rokar, about fifteen kilometers from the city of Pursat in western Cambodia. As I traveled by motorcycle to my village in the hot, steamy air, the sweat ran down my body like melting snow. I saw that everything had changed in the past twelve years: roads, houses, people. But when I went to the market in my village, I recognized many elders. They looked at me, wondering who I was. "My lord! Who are you?" they asked. I laughed and said, "Are you sure you've never seen me before?" I continued, "I am Darina, the oldest daughter of Teacher Siv and Chan Heang."

Everyone jumped up, hugged me, and pulled on my arms, saying, "You're so fat, my dear! You are so fat, so beautiful." They touched my body, admiring how plump I was; they had not recognized me at all. When I left Cambodia, I weighed less than 100 pounds. Now I weighed 150 pounds. The word *fat* that they repeated over and over bothered me. I had lived in America for a long time. In Cambodian culture, being *fat* meant you were rich and healthy. Clearly, I had enough money to buy good food to feed my body. People asked me if I had brought a "fat" medication along with me that they could have. Compared with me, they were so skinny, malnourished. Their skin was full of wrinkles.

After I said good-bye, I visited my old elementary school, where my father had taught thirty years ago. On the way from the market to the school, I saw only three small new houses. There were no big houses anymore. The road from the market to the school was just a trail overgrown with bushes. The school property turned out to be a banana farm.

∾

From the school to my house was a total jungle. It was very quiet. The river that crossed the village was so dry that I barely recognized it as a river. Finally, I walked to the property where my house used to be. What was left was only flat, dry land, the earth cracked into pieces like a puzzle. A few unhealthy bamboo bushes stood like fence and stared at me like a statue. I sat down in the middle of the property and tried to imagine my house, my parents, my siblings, and the wonderful trees that used to be there. I heard nothing, not even the sound of crickets, only the pulsating silence of the steamy heat. The rice field around my house had dried up. A couple of skinny old cows stood in it, looking for green grass.

The tamarind tree that used to comfort me when I had a hard time at school, that I hid behind when I played peekaboo with my friends, that served as a shelter to protect people from killing and executions, this giant tree had been cut down and chopped up. Only about two feet of its big trunk remained, charred and burnt.

I walked to a place where I used to come and look at my house and village from a distance. I remembered the day twenty-five years earlier when I had ridden my bike home from high school in Pursat and stopped here to watch my siblings and neighbors run toward me, welcoming me home. I closed my eyes and tried to imagine that day. My village was surrounded then by acres of green and gold rice fields, tall palm trees, coconut trees, banana trees, and slender bamboo. The flowing river crossed the middle of the village. There were many small and large houses with golden roofs. Two strong bulls pulled an oxcart, carrying a heavy load of rice under the hot sun. Birds flew from one place to another. The joyful sound of children's laughter rang out in the distance. A dog barked to warn the owner of his house that there was a stranger out front. Horses, cows, and buffalo rested under tall shade trees. I saw the red roof of my own house, shaded by banana trees, jackfruit trees, and bamboo swaying back and forth.

Now my village was a ghost town. Not only were there no people or houses left, but there were no birds flying, no wind bringing fresh air, no tree leaves blowing. No rooster crowed. No brown squirrel jumped from one coconut tree to another. The river had dwindled to a trickle, full of bamboo leaves and dirty water.

Before I left Cambodia, my grandmother had warned me, "If you leave, you can never come back." In a way, she was right. I had come back, but not to the same country I had left. And I was not the same, either. I was a professional woman living in the United States, far from the traditional role of my mother's expectations, far from the life I knew as a girl growing up in that wonderful, terrible place. But I am a Cambodian woman who lived in that past, and carried it into the future, and now give this memoir back to my children and others who want to understand the life of a survivor of the Cambodian genocide.

Never Come Back

ॐ

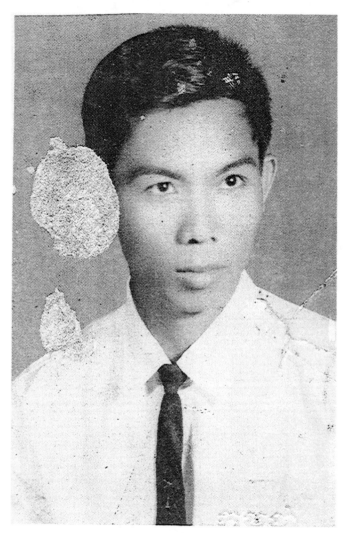

My father, Cheng Siv, in 1972

CHAPTER I

Family

My mother's long laugh sounded like water pouring from a clay pot. Her jokes, which everybody remembered and repeated, were slyly implanted with advice or a lesson. She had a bright happy face, a smile of love, kindness, and generosity. Standing five feet tall, she was light skinned and a little chubby for her size, which showed that she was rich. She had an oval face and permed hair cut in the style of the 1960s. Her brown eyes, which lay deep under heavy eyelids, indicated that she was second-generation Chinese-Cambodian. All the villagers loved her. They called her "teacher's wife."

My mother, Chan Heang, was born and raised in the village of Kompong Rokar, about fifteen kilometers from the city of Pursat in western Cambodia. She was the oldest of six children. Her father, Mr. Ty, was a first generation Chinese-Cambodian. As a boy, he refused to speak Chinese because he did not want to become a businessman as his father wished, as was expected of a Chinese boy. Ty chose instead to work as a farmer and fisherman.

My mother's mother, Mrs. Huot Horn, managed the finances and the house, including the family's outside properties. In the eyes of her children, she was the most strict and authoritarian mother in the world. They followed her rules as a Buddhist monk obeys the eightfold path. Although she did not have a formal education, she had learned the local laws and regulations from her father, who was an assistant deputy in the local government.

She knew how to resolve a fight between neighbors, where to find a lawyer, who to see to report a robbery.

In early 1948, when my mother was eight years old, her father struggled with an unknown disease that caused his leg to become paralyzed. Chan Heang was forced to quit school in the fourth grade to help take care of her father and her younger siblings. While her mother worked outside in the rice fields, Chan Heang prepared breakfast for her brothers and sisters, cooked lunch at noon, cleaned the house, carried water, and cut wood. If she did not complete her chores, she was disciplined by her mother.

My father, Siv, was born in Kandal Province, on an island chain called Konk Anlong Chin. He was a handsome man who stood five foot nine. His bony face and dark skin did not reveal his Chinese heritage, but his name did. Siv's father, Mr. Cheng, was a first-generation Chinese-Cambodian, with light skin and a calm, sweet, gentle personality. He worked as a farmer. Siv's mother, Mrs. Sdeng, was slim and aggressive, very talkative and very bossy. Siv's father valued education very highly. He sent Siv and his younger brother, Siv Jr., to study with Buddhist monks at a temple in Phnom Penh, the capital of Cambodia.

∾

Again and again throughout my childhood, my father told us about how hard he had struggled to reach his educational goals. He had to live apart from his family. At night, he sat under an oil lamp to read and do his homework, and when the monks turned off the lamp, he sometimes read by the light of incense sticks. In his spare time, he helped clean the temple, shopped for food with the monks, and washed clothes for them. The monks were very strict. Sometimes they beat him and his brother. Siv Jr. lost patience with them. He gave up his education and returned home to become a farmer. My father stayed in Phnom Penh and continued his studies with the monks; he also took classes in nursing at a school outside the temple. During the summers, he went home to help on his family's farm.

❧

In 1955, my father became a teacher. The Ministry of Education assigned him to teach in Battambang Province, and later in Kanh Chor, a village in Pursat Province. He stayed with his uncle, Mr. Touk, in Kahn Chor. One day, his parents visited and told Siv that it was time to start looking for a wife. His uncle took Siv's parents to a village near Kompong Rokar, not far from my mother's village, in search of a bride for Siv.

Unluckily, their search proved fruitless. They had come on bicycle, and it was a long way to return to Kanh Chor so late in the evening. Siv's uncle decided to stop overnight at the house of some old friends—my mother's parents. It was a very dark night. A petrol lamp shone dimly through the open window of the wooden house. In the kitchen, a slim eighteen-year-old girl wearing a dark navy blouse prepared food for the unexpected guests. A gentle wind blew in the window, bringing in the fresh air of the countryside and lifting the girl's long black hair from her face. She came into the room where the guests were talking with her parents and looked for just the right spot to put the hot, spicy soup on the red straw mat. Then she disappeared; tradition held that a young woman could not be in the room with guests unless it was necessary. My father's uncle got a quick glance at her and regretted that she couldn't stay.

"Is she your daughter, my friend?" he whispered. He could not wait for my grandparents to introduce her.

"Yes," my grandmother answered, then left him on the balcony with my father's parents to enjoy their late supper.

Outside, the full moon, rising just above the forest line, cast a dim ray over the village, like a thin cloth covering the dark of the night. The softly blowing wind kept the mosquitoes and other insects away from the guests. The crickets' singing mixed with the calls of night birds flying back and forth looking for food. Dogs barked at the other side of the village.

After clearing the mat where the guests had eaten, Chan Heang's parents chatted with my father's uncle, whom they had not seen for a long time. After a while, Mr. Cheng spoke. "We have come a long way to look for a wife for my son, who works as a teacher in Kanh Chor," he said. "We found your daughter here. We would like to engage her to our son. What do you think? I apologize for the short notice, but we come from far away."

"You want to engage my daughter at midnight—I never heard of such a thing!" my grandmother exclaimed. She and my grandfather left to discuss it. After they talked, my grandmother went to her father for advice. She also prayed before reaching a final decision; she believed in faith and destiny. Finally, she approved the engagement. But my mother knew nothing of it until a week before the wedding. She did not even have a chance to ask who the groom was. Neither my mother nor my father had a choice in the matter; nor were they allowed to tell their parents how they felt about getting married.

In my parents' generation, weddings lasted three days. The first day was the groom's parade, the second day was the wedding, and the third day was the reception. For his groom's parade, my father had to walk thirty kilometers from Kanh Chor, where he lived, to the bride's house in Kompong Rokar. My grandmother told me later that my father had complained about the long distance. And his uncle teased him that his bride was a cripple. But Siv could not abandon his responsibility without disgracing his family.

My father and mother saw each other for the first time on the second day of their wedding. My father was very happy because my mother was a beautiful bride, not a cripple like his uncle said. Ta Achar, the elder who was in charge of the wedding, had to stop my father from following my mother into her room that night. They had to complete the ceremony before the honeymoon.

After the wedding, my mother and father settled in Kompang Rokar. The villagers felt blessed to have my father as both a teacher and the village doctor. They were surprised to learn that he also farmed—in Cambodia, when someone became a teacher, it meant that he did not want to be a farmer. My father taught the villagers how to plant vegetables all year round, as he had learned on the island where he grew up. My grandmother worried that my mother might not handle her job as a housewife properly. It was not doing a job but learning how to get along with each other that was most important.

(Left to right) My father, sister Dasina, brother Darinal, and me.
This picture was taken at Tasknauk Elementary School in 1964.

Darina in first grade

CHAPTER 2

The Teacher's Daughter

IN 1957, A YEAR AFTER MY PARENTS GOT MARRIED, I was born under a bright full moon around nine o'clock. It was the year of the rooster, so everyone believed that I would be lucky and not have to work very hard to make money when I grew up. My father named me Soa after the day I was born, a Saturday. I don't know where Darina came from. I was the first granddaughter in the family. My grandmother was young, only thirty-six. I was surrounded and adored by aunts, uncles, great-aunts, and especially by my parents. In Cambodian culture, the first daughter is a treasure because she can help her mother with chores.

My mother complained about the traditional childbirth. For seven days after labor, a woman was supposed to eat very hot, spicy foods and drink a special wine mixed with medicinal herbs. My grandmother had preserved this special wine for a long, long time in preparation for the day her daughter would have a baby. The new mother also had to "stay on the grill"—under her bed, a pot of herbs simmered over warm charcoals. After seven days, my mother was free from this tradition.

My parents built a house after my brother was born, in 1959. It was a very big house, about 3,500 square feet, made of wood. It had a balcony in the front, a living room, bedroom, and kitchen. The house was by a rice field next to my grandparents' home.

In 1962, at the age of five, I started first grade. I was very young compared to my classmates, who were seven to ten years old.

Since public education was not compulsory in Cambodia, children did not start school at any particular age. It was up to each family to decide when or if their kids would go to school.

I had many girlfriends at school—and stories or nicknames for all of them. Mony was a smart rabbit-girl who had stolen a wise man's brain; Sivan, with her sharp, pointed nose and white skin, may have been reincarnated from a lost French colonist; Siv Yi was born in a hurry and forgot to take her extra leg bones, so she was shorter than the rest of us; Chou was a Chinese girl whose pig eyes made it hard to tell if she was falling asleep or staring at me; Oeun, a virtuous girl, rarely opened her mouth to engage in conversation or smile, but it was thunder or lightning if she did; Chay, a poor, pretty girl, believed that doing things without her parents' permission was a sin.

Another friend was Meng, a boy with skin so dark it looked like it had been burned in a fire. Sometimes I had to light a candle to see his face, but his bright teeth reflected the light when he laughed. To support his poor family, he worked as hard as a termite building its nest. Gnov, his brother, was fat and light skinned. He looked like a Chinese butcher but ran fast like a rat. Sep, a skinny girl, was a good swimmer and diver and liked to bite other kids' legs, like a flounder. Ee was an aggressive girl who bit like a mosquito and moved as fast as a cat stealing fish from the grill. Tong was an owl girl whose family owned mango trees. She gave me mangos to bring to my father so she could avoid a spanking at school. Unfortunately for Tong, I never brought the mangos to him. I ate them all.

Most of my friends were poor. They did not have any free time. They went to school with me in the morning and went home for lunch. After lunch, they looked for wood for cooking, carried water to put in the jar, took care of the cows or buffalo, then went back to school in the afternoon.

In contrast, my family had a maid to help my mother with chores and a man who helped my father with the farming. I did not have to carry water, look for wood, or take care of animals. Nonetheless, my mother trained me to be a good Cambodian girl. When I was six, she taught me how to cook, clean the house and kitchen, and take care of my younger siblings.

My mother also expected me to be a traditional Cambodian girl—polite, gentle, virtuous, and quiet, like Serr, who lived next door. People always praised her and said that she should have been born in my place. But I was the opposite: a tomboy who rebelled against the traditional culture. I climbed trees. I ran as fast as a lizard so that my feet almost didn't touch the ground. I went from my house to the other end of the village to see what all the villagers were doing. I liked to do boys' jobs to show that I was strong, physically and emotionally. I was their referee when they boxed. I played games with the boys and fought them if I had to. I took care of cows, cut leaves, and looked for wood. If an elder asked me for fruit, I would climb a tree and pick tamarind or mango or coconut.

At night, after washing the dishes and putting my little sister to sleep, I played hide and seek with other kids in the village under the moonlight. We did not have electricity. I loved to catch the fireflies that flew blinking and blinking around my grandmother's pond. I did not stop playing outside until I heard my mother's voice calling for me. When I did something I wasn't supposed to do, my mother pulled my ears or beat me. When I did wrong at school, my father punished me. But no matter what, I never gave up my active life outdoors.

I knew all the villagers' houses. One morning, as I was walking through the village as usual, I came upon an old lady who had fainted and fallen to the ground. I ran to my father for help. He gave her a couple of injections and some vitamins to take. Another time, a man knocked on our door at midnight and asked my father to help his wife, who had a very high fever. My father prepared his bag with his syringe and medicines. I asked if I could go with him, but he refused. After he left, I sneaked out and followed him. I ran behind him through a rough rice field that had just been harvested. I fell down. My father heard the noise and asked, "Who's that?"

"It's me, Rina."

"What are you doing here?"

"I want to go with you, Dad!" I said.

He pulled my hand and told me to walk behind him. After that, I always went with my father to treat people who needed help.

My father believed in the Western way of treating illness. Although he was my grandmother's favorite son-in-law, one thing he did not like about her was that she was a spirit caller. He tried to prove to her that Western treatments worked more effectively than spirit calling. But the hospital did not have enough doctors, and medical supplies were limited.

I knew very well how the spirit caller worked. Many times I had watched my grandmother when she practiced. I served as a messenger, bringing people to her, and I communicated with spirits myself. Sometimes I persuaded the spirit to bring me some food that I wanted, such as an expensive variety of banana. But I had to do this secretly, otherwise I would get a spanking from my father.

In addition to my playmates at school and in the village, I had other friends: the tamarind trees that let me lie on their branches and pick their fruit; the mango trees that provided shade like an umbrella for me to sit under while reading books or reciting lessons; the flowers—kravan, jasmine, hibiscus, and champa—to put in my long hair; the river that supplied cold clear water to cool my body; the sunset whose long rays I watched before he said good-bye to the world; the sunrise that brought hope and strength and added to my age one day at a time; the sky that was too high for me to reach, but was always there to reassure me; the wind that wrapped my body like a soft, gentle blanket for my truest security; the birds that sang with many different voices in a song that never ended.

My father woke up every morning at three o'clock to plow the rice field. I got up at five o'clock and cooked rice soup for the family's breakfast. After cleaning up, I put food out on the balcony for my bird friends. On the way to school, I stopped many times to watch the birds play, sing, and fly. Sometimes I was punished for being late. In the evening, if I could not stay outside to watch the sunset, I looked out the window instead. I listened to the sound of oxcarts carrying loads of rice, the sounds of cows, buffalo, and birds, until my mother screamed at me to close the window.

At night, I opened a window to let in the fresh air while I studied. A tree branch blew back and forth across the window, a soft rustling noise that made me lose my concentration. Usually my father came and closed the window, and I knew it was time for him to give me lessons. I wasn't smart enough for him. He wanted me to be the number one student in the classroom. But I did not understand mathematics. I did not do as well as he expected, and he hit me.

Late at night, I cried because my father hit me. I talked to that tree branch outside the window. Why couldn't he save me from my father's spankings? I thought the tree was luckier than I.

❧

In 1962, I was in second grade, my sister Dasina was born, and I was struck with hepatitis B, which gave me black spots all over my body, especially on my face. The spots around my mouth looked like a mustache. My grandparents, uncles, and aunts teased me and called me "black" instead of my name. They focused their attention on my sister, whom they adored. They called her Mouch—meaning "cutie" or "charming." I loved my sister, but I could not stand being put down. I became even more stubborn. I was not ashamed of how I looked. My mother begged me to study hard. She said that no one would want to marry me, that she would have to buy a groom for me because I was so ugly. I was sad, and also very angry.

I almost died of hepatitis. My mother fed me by dropping rice soup and water into my mouth. My father had to lift me up and carry me to the bathroom. I was jaundiced and very skinny. I did not go to school for days. I rested at home with my mother and my younger siblings. Curled up in the crook of my mother's arm, covered with a blanket, I watched the heavy rain drip through a rainspout from the roof into the big jar where we collected water. The soft music of the falling rain put me to sleep.

The villagers believed that my illness stemmed from a sin I had committed in a previous life, or from someone's curse on me. They felt sorry for my parents. My father treated me with his Western medicine, and my health improved toward the end of the school year. The black spots did not disappear, but I was finally able to go back to school.

In the summer, when school was out, my father brought me to Battambang Province to look for ways to treat the spots on my skin. We saw a Japanese doctor and an herbalist, but nothing worked. Every summer after that, we traveled somewhere else, looking for a new skin treatment.

I entered third grade in 1964. It was a bad year for me because my father was my teacher. He asked me questions before he asked the other students. Among forty-five students in the classroom, I was ranked number forty-five. Every day, I got a beating. I spent more time thinking about how to avoid my father's long stick than about the assignments he gave me.

One day, I had the idea to put my baby pillow across my backside so that when my father hit me it would not hurt as much. As usual, that day at school I was beaten. This time, my father's long stick whipping me sounded different. I did not cry like I usually did. My father was suspicious. He felt my butt and pulled out the pillow. This time, he would not let me get away. He hit me more and more. I cried and watched as blood rushed from my forearms and dropped onto the ground. The blood spread onto my palms like ketchup from a broken bottle. The other students looked at me with pity, but they could not help me.

∾

When I went back to my desk, I thought that I must not be his real daughter. Maybe I was picked up from the trash, like everyone said. I stopped crying just as the bell rang. It was time to go home. Everybody rushed out of the classroom and ran toward their homes. I was the last one to leave the building. I was not running. I walked very slowly across the rice field with my face toward the ground. I wanted to run away, but I didn't know where to go. Everyone in the village knew me, and they would bring me home. I talked with my bird friends along the way and told them how lucky they were to be born as a bird. I looked across the rice field to the horizon, as far away as hope was to me.

As I neared my house, I came to my best friend, the tamarind tree. I climbed the tree and lay down on a big strong branch that made a bed for me. Exhausted, I fell asleep. I was awakened by a conversation.

"Do you see our daughter?"

"No."

"You must have hit her badly again!"

The one who answered walked away. Without moving, I peeked out and saw my mother sitting just below the branch where I lay. She talked to herself.

"Oh! My dear daughter, it is noon. You must be very hungry. Where are you? How can I find you?"

Now I knew that my mother loved and cared for me. I was her real daughter. I wanted to reveal myself but I was not strong enough to come out of the tree.

My mother took a deep breath and pulled out her kramar (scarf) to cover her head and protect it from the hot sun. After she left, I climbed down and walked home. My mother kept my lunch waiting for me. I was very hungry. I ate all the food without saying a word.

❧

In 1965, my fourth brother, Nara, was born, and I was excited to enter fourth grade, with a new teacher. But he and my father had the same teaching style—hitting. The new teacher was worse than my father. I tried to avoid his beatings by studying hard, especially the French language. The next year, in fifth grade, I had a new teacher, who did not punish me as much. He respected me as the "daughter of Teacher Siv." In his class, my grades improved. I was ranked among the top ten students, which made me very proud. French and Khmer language were my favorite subjects, as well as history, geography, and science. I still had a hard time with math.

In Cambodia, students had to pass a national examination to enter high school, which started in sixth grade. Two of my uncles were in the same class as me. One uncle, Ty Kim Toc, failed the exam three times. The other uncle, Ty Kim Tav, failed twice. They both teased me that I would never make it.

I passed the national examination the first time. My parents were very proud. At age eleven, I was the youngest student ever to pass the national exam. I saved my father's reputation by passing. And I would get to go to high school in the city.

My father sat me down and talked with me: "Going to high school requires a lot of attention and concentration," he said. "From now on, I am not going to hit you anymore. I will leave you alone and I won't bother you, but you must study hard. Education is your life."

After my father left, my mother came into the room and sat by my side. She looked directly at me. She put her hand on my shoulder and said, "Honey, education is very important. It will lead to self-sufficiency. I would not recommend that you depend on a husband's income. Men want to marry beautiful girls, and . . . you don't have that kind of beauty. But education will prevent you from being put down by others. The thief can steal your property—your bike, jewelry, things—but not your education. A rat cannot ruin it, a spider cannot make a home of it, and termites cannot use it in their nest. No one can steal your education from you, my dear."

My parents' speeches gave me a lot of ideas about my life and future, which I did not yet fully understand. I was not ready to grow up. I wanted to play in the village with my friends and enjoy nature. Going to high school in the city would be a difficult change, but I was glad for the freedom from discipline. And I still had two more months to be with my friends and play outside.

My friends, who were not able to continue their education, told me how lucky I was to be the teacher's daughter. Oh, my dear friends, you'll never know how much pressure I felt being the teacher's daughter!

CHAPTER 3

Teenage Life

ONLY THREE GIRLS—MONY, SIVAN, AND I—and a couple of boys passed the national exam to enter high school. I was scared to leave my village and go to a big school in the city. But the expectations of my parents, extended family, and the villagers gave me a strong incentive to pursue higher education.

I looked forward to enjoying the summer with my friends and siblings, but instead, my parents sent me to stay with my aunt Ny, in Lor Lok Sar, about twenty miles away. Ny's husband was a teacher who had recently graduated from the Faculty of Pedagogy in Phnom Penh, and my father hoped he would help me prepare for sixth grade. My father worried that I would have a hard time keeping up with all the subjects in high school. I did not want to go to Lor Lok Sar, but I had no choice.

My uncle had a fourteen-year-old brother who had also recently passed the national exam. His name was Kheun. He was about five feet tall, with dark skin and curly hair. He was funny and a good singer. My aunt asked Kheun to watch me while she went out—she was afraid that I might run back home. I did not want Kheun to be my boss. I gave him a hard time by not following his directions. I hated the way he looked at me, followed me, and controlled me.

The sixth week was my last week with my aunt and uncle. Kheun sang a song for me called "Long Black Hair." He dedicated it to me.

Long black hair, always shining into my eye,
Long black hair, combed to say good-bye,
Forever, if you cut it, you will make me cry,
Because I want you keep it, before you say good-bye.

I paid no attention to his song. My soul had already gone home. I dreamed about my brothers and sisters, my parents, my friends, the rice fields, the river, the tree where I used to climb. Hooray! I'm going home, I'm going home. I wanted to say this word over and over. I would have freedom tomorrow.

As for Kheun, he felt sad all day. I thought he would be happy because it was a big job to be in charge of me when I always gave him a hard time. I did not see him when I left.

∾

In 1968, my first year in seventh grade, my parents sent me to live with my uncle Hann, my mother's younger brother. He worked as a policeman in the city of Pursat. He was married and had three children, ages seven, five, and three. I had my own room at the back of his small house. Each month my father gave my uncle a fifty-pound bag of rice, dried food, and 100 riels. My father also bought me a brand-new bicycle to ride to school and to come home on weekends.

On Saturdays, I had class in the morning. I could not sit still. I couldn't wait to get out of class and go home to my village. A one-hour class stretched on forever. Finally, it was over. I rushed to my uncle's house and peddled my bike home.

The villagers cried out to welcome me. My friends ran up and pulled my bike out of my hands to try it out. A sister of a friend ran to my house and told my parents and siblings that I was home. I had to push through the crowd to get home. I stopped and chatted with one friend and then another. They asked me how I liked the city—maybe I had too much fun there and forgot them? I was very anxious to see my family.

In the evening, I sat my younger brother on my bike with me and rode to visit my friends and neighbors. They asked me all kinds of questions about the city and school. Everyone, young and old, listened quietly. They thought I was lucky to go to high school in the city.

But my life was not the same. My old best friends treated me differently. The only thing that did not change was nature. The trees were still green and healthy and moved back and forth when the wind blew, as if saying hello. Birds jumped from one branch to another and waved at me with their wings clapping. Fresh air still comforted me when I lay down on the tamarind branch. The fields were a big green carpet for me to sit on.

During that school year, I found it very difficult to adjust to the living situation with my uncle. I had to do more chores than I expected, which affected my school performance. My parents saw this and decided to build a house for me to live in the city. It would be there for my younger siblings, too.

In the summer of 1968, my new house was built in Phom Cham Kar Chak, about a kilometer from my high school and the market in Pursat. It was a three-bedroom house. My father moved to Pursat and began teaching at North Elementary School, while my mother continued to live in the village with my younger siblings.

It was a big change for my family. It seemed like we had two families instead of one. My sister Dasina, my brother Rinal, my brother Rino, my brother Nara, and I lived with my father in the new house.

1969 was a wonderful year for me. I felt like the caterpillar that turned into a butterfly. One day, the black spots on my face and body completely disappeared, after six years of shame. I was crazy about my new looks. Everyone wanted to make friends with me. My parents were overjoyed to see me looking as beautiful as everyone else.

It was not only my physical self that healed. My ability to

think and my knowledge grew, and I discovered that I was talented in literature. Every day I wrote children's stories and poems. I neglected everything else to write. My parents discouraged me from pursuing a life as a writer. They believed a writer would never make a good living. My friends made jokes about me. They called me "the legendary girl writer." I had a pile of stories.

In October 1969, I sent my first story to a radio station in Phnom Penh that broadcast children's stories every Wednesday morning. To avoid punishment, I used a pen name, Duong Ratha, and my school address. The story, "Kids Helping Kids," was about doing homework as a team with friends.

I listened to the children's program on the radio every Wednesday, but I never heard my story. I waited and waited. At the same time, I kept sending more stories—"A Brave Poor Boy," "A Girl and an Old Man," "The Rich Kid and the Blind Dog," "A Blind Mother Raised a Good Child," "The Poor Girl Can Learn," "The Baby and the Rabbit," "A Snake Becomes a Monk."

Whatever I saw or observed, I turned into stories, which I enjoyed writing very much. Most of my stories came to me when I was kneeling, looking down at the floor, and saying nothing for one or two hours while my parents preached. My mind was busy imagining stories and remembering them. Now it was time to share them with other kids.

One week passed, followed by a second and a third. I heard nothing from the children's story program. Finally, I gave up. Then, on January 6, 1970, my father was testing a new battery for the radio and he tried out different stations. Accidentally, he turned to the children's story program—and they were broadcasting my first story, "Kids Helping Kids"! I was in the kitchen putting out food for lunch. I was excited and thrilled to hear my story on the air. I couldn't even find words to express my feelings.

"It's a good idea for kids to help each other with their homework. I never thought about that!" my father whispered. He was impressed that Miss "Duong Ratha" had sent her story to air on the radio.

Later, six other stories of mine aired on consecutive Wednesdays. At my high school, students were curious to know who Duong Ratha was. In just two weeks, I received thirty or forty letters from listeners—students, nurses, soldiers—from different provinces. Some included pictures, thank-you cards, and letters of admiration. Wow! I felt great. I was very popular, but I did not have enough money to buy stamps to write back to my listeners. My parents were right that I would never make a living as a writer.

CHAPTER 4

Changes

ON MARCH 18, 1970, GENERAL LON NOL carried out a military coup on the royalist regime of Norodom Sihanouk. Lon Nol was a general in Sihanouk's regime, which began in 1953. Backed by the United States government under President Richard Nixon, Lon Nol deposed Sihanouk out of power when the prince was out of the country on a trip to France. After the bloodless coup, Lon Nol declared the kingdom of Cambodia to be the Khmer Republic. (The Khmer Rouge used the date of the coup, March 18, 1970, to identify people who fought with them against the Republic government as "Old People" or "Based People"—*Mola-thaan* in the Cambodian language).

Many people in the rural areas of Cambodia supported Prince Sihanouk, who was loved by Khmer elders. He was less popular among educated people and those who lived in the cities. Prince Sihanouk was known as the "father of national independence," "the father of national health," "the father of the budget," etc. The prince's picture hung on the wall in almost every Cambodian house. A country without Prince Sihanouk was like a house without a father.

Sihanouk went to China and declared the coup illegal. He called on the Cambodian people to leave their homes and join forces with the Communist Khmer Rouge (literally, "red Khmer") soldiers in the jungle and take up arms and fight against the traitor Lon Nol. Some people believed that Cambodia would not see peace as long as there was no king to rule the country. They trusted Prince Sihanouk with all their heart. They sat around the household radio to listen to his voice on a Chinese radio station every evening.

Prince Sihanouk's National Liberation Front was aligned with the Khmer Rouge and the Russian, Chinese, and North Vietnamese governments. The Khmer Rouge received military assistance from North Vietnam and China. Khmer Rouge soldiers were trained by Viet Cong forces from North Vietnam. The Khmer Rouge occupied rural areas of Cambodia, where support for Sihanouk was strong.

At the beginning of the war, Lon Nol's Khmer Republic government was backed by the U.S. government and the South Vietnamese. The U.S. government provided military aid indirectly through Vietnam and Thailand to support Nol's Republican soldiers. The Republic's ground troops trained in South Vietnam and Thailand.

Compared with other provinces, Pursat Province did not have a lot of protests in support of the king. But people were uncertain about living without Prince Sihanouk.

After the Vietcong invasion of Cambodian territory, some students at my school protested against the Vietnamese civilians who lived in Cambodia. The protesters marched from Pursat High School to the market, holding signs reading "Vietnam out of Cambodia." The students and other protesters went wild—they screamed at Vietnamese merchants, destroyed their property, and scared them into closing their stores and running for shelter.

In April 1970, just before the Cambodian New Year, it was chaos in the Pursat market. Two Vietnamese toddlers cried and ran naked across the street, looking for their parents. Seeing this, I walked away from the crowd, stood in the shade of a nearby tree, and decided to stay outside the picket line. I did not think it was right to target the Vietnamese people who had lived in this town for generations. How was I going to deal with my classmate Kim Ouk, with whom I had held hands, played, talked, and smiled every day?

❧

A week later, the whole class turned against my friend Kim Ouk. They did not play with her, talk to her, or even smile at her. I was trapped. I did not want to consider Kim Ouk my enemy, but I did not want my other classmates to think I supported the Vietcong either. I treated her the same as my best friend.

The school recruited male students to train for what was called "commando" duty, to protect the school against a Vietcong attack. Commando shelters were built next to schools. The commando guarded the school entrance twenty-four hours a day.

In ninth grade, classes were divided into two concentration areas: agriculture and science. Science included mathematics, physics, chemistry, and hand crafts (for girls). Agriculture concentrated on how to plant rice, languages, history, and geography. Agriculture required a lot of time for experiments outside the classroom.

The major problem was that the rice paddy needed more water. We had only one well to use for the entire high school. The commandos also used this well for cooking and showering. Pulling the water out of the well was very hard. My solution was to ask a commando to help. The commandos were very kind and generous.

Going through puberty at age fourteen, I turned out to be a pretty girl. At five foot two inches, I was slim, taller than most girls, and faster than my classmates. My face was very smooth—I rarely had a pimple. My long, straight black hair was shiny and healthy. It covered my back like a dark silk cloth.

I was outgoing, friendly, curious, and funny. I knew students, both male and female, from seventh to twelfth grade. I asked older students for help with my math, physics, and chemistry, and they agreed without hesitation. I was attracted to the older male students, who were quiet and talked less. In contrast, most of my girlfriends strictly followed the code of conduct for girls. They were quiet, walked slowly and gently, and hardly ever talked to male students inside or outside the classroom.

In May 1971, I met a twenty-year-old senior, a handsome, quiet, gentle young man named Tep Sung Vuth, who was very smart in mathematics. He was from another town. His mother had died when he was young, and his father had remarried. Vuth had thirteen siblings. After school, he worked as a private mathematics tutor and a commando.

Vuth helped me carry water out of the well every day for my rice paddy project. We became friends. We talked and made jokes, and he helped me with my homework. I liked that he was so understanding. But this friendship did not last long. At the end of the school year, two weeks before heading to Battambang Province to take the national baccalaureate examination, Vuth handed me a letter, a letter that ended our friendship and started a new chapter called "love." His beautiful handwriting described his life in an orphanage at a young age; my beauty, which made his steel heart soft and weak; and a proposal of love full of hope for the future. Finally, he asked me for a hopeful word, YES, a word that would inspire him to pass his examination.

I was fourteen and he was twenty. I did not want to end this friendship. My heart said "yes" but my mouth would not open to let this word out. I felt trapped. School would be out in just a week. I was very anxious to see Vuth, especially to find out about his exam.

∾

Two days before school ended, Vuth gave me a postcard, which he bought for me in Battambang Province. It was a picture of a man standing up behind a beautiful lady who was sitting on a chair. The man was giving the woman a red rose. Vuth told me sadly that he had failed his exam. I felt sorry for him. But he would have a chance to take a second test in two months. I hoped he would pass his second exam.

The high school was on vacation for two months. During this time, I had to take care of my siblings, cook, and clean the house and clothes. Once a week, I went to my village to visit my mother and younger siblings. Even though I saw my old friends and visited my favorite places in the village, I could not ease my feelings of sadness, frustration, and depression. I had no one to share my feelings with. Even if I had, I was afraid to—it would mean trusting an outsider with myself and my family.

I wanted to see Vuth and find out how he was doing. There was no way to see him that summer. I was supposed to behave properly in public and not show any sexual feelings toward a man. Every possible solution I came up with turned out to be a dead end. The rigid Cambodian culture prohibited a girl from having a boyfriend because it would disgrace the family reputation. The burden was especially heavy on me as a first daughter. The first daughter must be a role model for the other siblings. If I did something wrong, it would affect my whole family.

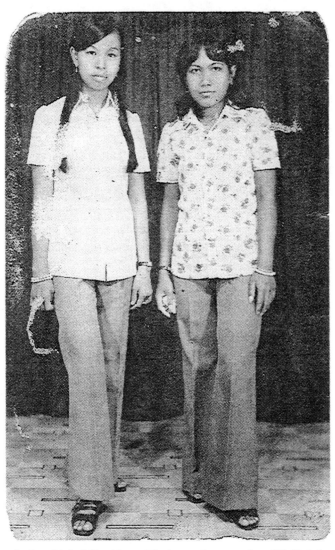

Darina with best friend Bunny Yim in 1972. Bunny was later killed in jail.

CHAPTER 5

A Broken Heart

THE FIRST DAY OF SCHOOL, September 9, 1971, was a great day for me. I was a bird released from its cage. The first thing I did was look for Vuth to see how he had been in the past months. His commando shelter had new students in charge. I saw one of Vuth's friends walking by me.

"How is Vuth doing?" I asked him.

"After failing his second exam, he joined the navy," he answered. For minutes I was totally unconscious. I was finally awakened by the ring of the school bell.

My heart was broken. I blamed myself for letting him fail his exam. His absence made me feel guilty. I asked his best friend if Vuth had left any message or letter for me. None. He left to join the navy without a trace. No one had an address where I could reach him.

The next couple of weeks passed very slowly. I lost weight, became very depressed, and dreamed about Vuth day and night. Every day was like living in darkness. I had no one to turn to. I asked the wind to bring my message to Vuth that I loved him very much.

∽

One day, one of my classmates claimed that she was Vuth's cousin. She told me that Vuth was very anxious to see me, but had no way to reach me. He was also afraid of my parents. He was despairing because he had been an A student and he failed his second examination. He felt like a loser. He was not good enough for me. He had started abusing alcohol. Then he decided to join the navy. Pain squeezed my heart. It hurt so bad, like my heart was torn apart.

During the first quarter of school, my grades fell in all subjects, which worried my father. I had to take a national exam to be able to enter my junior year. I tried to take one day at a time to cope with the pain. I found ways to deal with it. But it was hard to face the fact that Vuth was not in Pursat anymore. My only hope was that one day he would come back to see me.

January was rice harvest season. In many rural areas of the country, Khmer Rouge soldiers and Republican soldiers were fighting over territory. The Khmer Rouge's strategy was very wise. When they captured the rural areas, they built relationships with the villagers to gain trust and popularity. They did not hurt or touch any civilian property. If they picked one hot pepper, they put money by the plant.

In contrast, the Republican soldiers, supported by American and South Vietnamese soldiers, destroyed houses, bombed rice supply warehouses, shot animals, and cut down trees. They raped and tortured villagers accused of being affiliated with the Khmer Rouge.

The villagers were very fearful. My mother and younger siblings moved to live with me in the city after a bomb was dropped near their house. It was very sad to see the house empty, without people around.

With all the national events happening every day, my broken heart was getting better. Little by little, I was able to handle my life more easily. Still, I worried about Vuth constantly. I prayed for his safety.

At the end of the school year, I passed the national exam to go on to my junior year. My parents were so proud of me. But one thing they did not know was how painful it was for me to work to pass the exam while I had a broken heart.

∾

By 1972, my junior year, I felt completely recovered. I began to write children's stories again. In addition, I volunteered with the Khmer Red Cross Women's Association, run by the governor's wife. I made friends at school and outside of school—people of high rank, including officers, province ministers, and journalists. I went with them to distribute gifts to wounded soldiers in the hospitals. I had a chance to attend government meetings and discuss the management of the government. I challenged them about corruption and unfairness in the government. But the high-ranking officers did not take my arguments seriously. They thought I was just a kid and just a girl.

I also discussed political issues with my father. My mother complained that I was talking too much. She suggested that I shouldn't get involved in politics. In politics, she said, the only way you'd end up was "dead," because people used people. She advised me not to ever try to become a senator or house representative. Asking votes from people was something I should avoid.

The civil war was getting worst and worse. The Khmer Rouge captured most rural areas, which drove many refugees into the city. The city was full of people and very dirty. Some families became homeless. There was not enough food, shelter, clothing, or medicine. People contracted many diseases.

The Khmer Rouge cut off the rice supply through National Route 5, a major route to transport supplies from Phnom Penh to Pursat and Battambang. Sometimes, refugees supplies came from the air. There were robberies all over the place, day and night. It was never safe. Inflation skyrocketed. But workers' salaries did not cover the cost of living, which forced many teachers to protest against the government.

Compare to other families, my family had more than enough
to live. We could not live on my father's income like we used to,
however. My mother had her own business, transporting hogs
for wholesale. She could make as much money in one day as my
father earned in a month. I was busy counting money. My mother
never believed in putting money in a bank. In one year, we could
have made a mattress out of her money.

CHAPTER 6

An American Friend

IN THE LATE SUMMER OF 1974, the United States Consulate announced an offer of free English classes. They would be held at an office near National Route 5, a highway that ran from Phnom Penh to Battambang Province, cutting across Pursat Province. The class was offered to all provincial officers, deputies, ministers, and teachers. It was taught by an American consul.

My friends Thiny, Bunny, and I were very interested in taking this English class, but we could not get in. I asked my friend who was the provincial minister of information to bring the three of us to the class. The teacher introduced himself as Michael Inghim. Six feet tall, with brown hair, blue eyes, and a mustache, he came from Reston, Virginia. He would work in Pursat for six months. Because there were too many students the first day, he decided to do individual testing. More than half of the students, including my two friends, failed the test. I was the next one to take it, and I did not expect to pass. It was my lucky day. I could answer all his questions. I could come to the class.

Mike shared an office with his partner, Robert Basket, a native of West Virginia. There were also four Khmer staff: Ms. Bina (Mike's secretary), Ms. Sopha, Mr. Keth Be, and Mr. Nora.

I studied very hard and tried to practice conversation. My English improved rapidly. I was able to make conversation with Mike about everything. He told me that his parents were still living in Reston. His father worked as a veterinarian, and his mother was a housewife. He had three brothers. His older brother was in the Air Force in South Vietnam. This brother was married and had two children. Mike, the second child, was thirty-one years old, thirteen years older than me. He was single. His younger brother was crippled and lived with his parents. I remember that Mike asked me a question about a boyfriend. I didn't know what he meant. I told him that I had many friends who were boys!

One evening, it was raining so hard that I couldn't go home. I stayed in class and practiced English with Mike. He also allowed me to practice with him for an extra hour another day. "What do you want to do when you grow up?" he asked. "I want to be a secretary," I answered nervously. Mike asked his secretary to teach me how to type. Later, Mike became very busy and cut down his class hours.

My regular school was closed on and off due to a teachers' strike in protest of low salaries and skyrocketing inflation. This gave me time to practice English conversation with Mike and to learn to type. I also had a chance to learn more about the American lifestyle. Every evening, I came home and shared what I learned with my father. We had long discussions about American civilization and how our leaders should rebuild this poor country so that people's suffering would end. Often the discussions were interrupted by my mother, who did not want to hear me talking about politics.

Besides learning English, I signed up for a "political war" class that the governor organized, which was taught by high-ranking officers. I learned about the Communist theories used to brainwash people. The Communists said that rich people sucked blood from the poor by using them as their slaves. That was why the rich got richer and the poor got poorer. These messages were a hit with homeless people in the cities and poor farmers with no education. They happily joined the Khmer Rouge forces. They believed the slogan, "You will become an owner of yourself." The Communists believed they could bring the whole world into the Communist party.

At home, I shared these new ideas with my father. He also gave me some clues to look for in the people around me. He believed there were many Khmer Rouge spies around us. My relationship with my father became very close as I opened up more about my feelings and goals—except the boyfriend issue.

Every day, more refugees escaped from the Khmer Rouge zone. Every public place in the city—temples, schools, streets—was overcrowded and the new arrivals had no place to go for shelter. National Route 5 had been completely cut off by Khmer Rouge forces, who used land mines and bombs to destroy bridges. The supplies dropped from the air by Lon Nol's government were not adequate to meet the refugees' need. The price of rice, meat, and vegetables skyrocketed. People who had no money were forced to rob and kill each other. Many young girls from the countryside were kidnapped and sold as prostitutes. Government workers' monthly salaries were only enough to feed their families for a week. They had to find other ways to make money to support their families. Hospitals were overflowing with wounded soldiers and injured civilians, without medicine for treatment. Many schools in rural areas were closed. Students moved to the city to continue their education. They came from many different provinces across the country.

Compared with other places in Cambodia, Pursat was still peaceful. There was no bombing, shelling, or fighting in the city. The battles were far away. At night, a curfew was enforced from 8:00 P.M. to 7:00 A.M.

When I saw Mike, I asked him about the Communist regime. I told him I did not like the Khmer Rouge. I also told him that I wanted to visit the United States. Mike was happy to tell me about life in his hometown—the schools, shops, movie theaters, food, and parks—which helped me to dream about it more. Mike kindly offered to support my financial needs so I could continue to go to school. In addition, he asked his secretary, Bina, to train me in a secretarial job, filing, typing, and sorting. I felt that Mike was my best friend.

∾

As time passed, Mike talked about going back to the United States. His last day in Cambodia would be February 10, 1975. Two weeks before leaving, Mike asked me if I would go with him to Virginia. He talked about his mother, father, and brothers. He told me again that he was single, which I did not believe at all. In my country, I had never seen a bachelor that old. To convince me, he showed me his identification papers, which indicated that his mother was his insurance beneficiary. He also joked that if I did not go with him I would be married to the Khmer Rouge.

It was a very difficult decision for me. I told Mike how hard it was for me to decide, but I said I would ask my parents' permission. I would let him know the next day.

That evening, I told my father about my relationship with Mike and asked for permission to go to the United States with him. I was desperate to hear his answer. He was silent for only a moment. After taking a deep breath, he gave me a simple answer: "Yes! I permit you to go for the good of your future." I was very surprised. "But ask your mom also," he continued. After getting this assurance from my father, I was thrilled and excited and quickly ran to my mother. She shut me up even before I could even finish the question. "You! Go to the United States with an American?" she screamed, looking straight into my eyes with her eyes wide open. "What are you two up to? Ah! What kind of girl do you think you are? You are a Khmer girl—why do you want to run away with an American man? How long have you known him? I sent you to go to school, not to run way with a man to the U.S. You have black blood, you are not my daughter. If you dare to go with him, then go—but never return to see my funeral."

She went on and on. "Mother, I understand," I said. "Please, that's enough. I'm just asking for your permission, that's all." My explanation did not make her feel better, but instead was like pouring gasoline onto a wildfire. I let my mother continue her preaching as I walked away to do my chores.

I could not sleep that night. I thought about how I would tell Mike the next day. I did not want him to think I was a liar. I really wanted to go to the United States. At the same time, I tried to calm my disappointment. I could go with Mike if I wanted to. But looking back, it was impossible for me to ignore the strong bond that tied me to my family. It weighed more heavily on me than anything else.

I also knew that one day my country would collapse. I was scared of the brutality of the Khmer Rouge. I had heard stories from people who had escaped the Khmer Rouge zone about how the Khmer Rouge killed people by cutting their throats with palm leaves. They targeted people who were educated because they thought these people were more difficult to control.

But I wanted to die with my family. I did not want to run away to the United States and let my family suffer. That would go against the values my parents had taught me.

The next day, I went straight to Mike and gave him my answer. I explained to him about my culture, my family's values, and my current situation. Mike pleaded with me to trust him enough to leave my family. But he could not persuade me to go with him.

"You will be married to a Khmer Rouge soldier!" he yelled.

Finally, he asked me to do three things for him: learn English, become a secretary, and keep my long hair.

༄

On February 10, 1975, a light green Jeep with a diplomatic license plates drove slowly to take Mike and his belongings toward a private plane that waited for him at the small airport. I did not want to say good-bye to him because I did not want him to leave. If I could have paused the sun for another day, I would have. My heart felt the sound of the airplane taking off over my roof. I lay on the hammock and looked at the plane as it pumped fuel into a line of smoke that got farther and farther away . . . while the radio played a popular Carpenters song of the '70s, "Yesterday."

My high school classmates in February 1975, two months before the Khmer Rouge takeover.

CHAPTER 7

April 17, 1975

ON APRIL 17, 1975, THE KHMER ROUGE took control of Phnom Penh. We learned the news from an announcement on the radio. I was with friends at my teacher's house just outside Pursat. We were celebrating the New Year with food, music, and dancing. While we were dancing, the teacher's maid came over. "Sir! I'm sorry to interrupt you, but there's a lot of gunfire outside." Everyone quickly said good-bye and left.

At two o'clock that afternoon, as I was riding my bike home, I saw white flags, a symbol of peace, in front of every government office building. People cheered to welcome this new peace. Everybody thought that the war was over and now there would be peace, for which we had waited five years.

Some relatives were reunited now that the nation had become one. Everywhere people celebrated to show their acceptance of the new regime.

My grandparents and mother were so happy. I felt hopeless because I knew exactly what my country would become in the future. My father was worried, too. I explained to my grandparents that the Communist regime would not be any fun. They would force us to work hard and take away our freedom. No one believed me. My grandmother said I was too young to understand this victory. She ordered me to cook for the soldiers. I was very mad but couldn't say anything. I learned that we were called "New People" or "17 April." The Khmer Rouge were called "Old

People" or "18 March," for the date of Lon Nol's coup, when the Khmer Rouge had begun fighting the Republican government.

Later, people's mood changed. My mother started to worry, and she looked at her children with hopelessness. The schools closed. Cambodian money had no value. The markets were closed. In the chaos, people robbed stores for everything they could get for their family. Many patients at hospitals were sent home. People abandoned their regular work routine and waited for orders from the new government. Refugees who had been clustered in the city for so long were happy to return home. They walked, drove oxcarts, and carried their belongings, marching in a long line as if in a parade. They thought they had their freedom again. My parents prohibited me from going outside because they did not feel it was safe. People who stopped by our house talked about how the Khmer Rouge soldiers shot people who went against them. Everybody was very scared.

My father was busy taking care of the cows, pigs, chickens, and ducks around the house. Sometimes he stared at the animals with a sad expression on his face because he knew they would not belong to him in the future.

On April 18, at 10:00 A.M., gunfire sounded everywhere in the city of Pursat. The Communist soldiers—men, women, and kids as young as twelve, dressed in black clothes and black caps, with black scarves wrapped around their necks—walked through the city, carrying all kinds of weapons, and declared their victory. It looked just like an alien invasion. People could not hold themselves back—they stood up in front of their houses and celebrated this historical event.

The radio in Phnom Penh played the patriotic Communist music again and again. Communist soldiers moved through the city and asked people to give them their cars, bicycles, watches, motorcycles, oxcarts, and clothes.

I went up to my room and sat down on my bed, feeling depressed. I thought about Mike. I knew I would never see him again. Now we lived in two separate worlds, heaven and hell. I did not think I would survive the Communist regime. From what I had learned from my political class, discussions with Mike, and talking with people who had been in the Khmer Rouge zone, I knew how bad things would be. But I was happy to die with my family. As I looked through the window, I saw gun smoke floating high in the sky. I did not think I would have a chance to return to school again. I was bored. I missed my friends and my teachers so much.

On April 22, all the teachers and students were told to meet at the basketball court in front of my high school. My mother advised me to dress as a farmer. I walked instead of riding a bicycle. At the school, I got to see my friends and teachers again. I hugged my girlfriends Bunny and Thiny. We had a million things to share. It seemed that all our teachers had become our friends. We all asked each other where we were going. Most people had decided to go to Leach, a village about thirty-five kilometers from Pursat, because they were planning a revolution against the Khmer Rouge. Suddenly, the loud voice of a man with a microphone interrupted our discussion. He was a medium-sized man, wearing worn black clothes. He looked intelligent, like an educated person. He stood on the second-floor balcony of the building and started to inform us what would happen to us as students and teachers.

"My fellow friends! Our victory shows that farmers and workmen now are self-ruled. We do not have to work under the capitalists who suck the blood of our poor people. With empty hands we fought the imperialist Americans until we now have everything—victory! Now it is time to start to rebuild our country. We need your help. You have to clean out your old brain in order to receive our beautiful regime, which we have never had in our history. You will continue your education, but not in the school building, the old system. Instead you will learn to work in the rice fields to build yourselves up physically and psychologically.

We have endured a great loss during the war because of the Americans. If we work together, we can build this country to become one of the strongest and richest in the world. Rice farms are our country's major resource. That's how you, as students and teachers, can join our labor and contribute to our regime. Now, when you leave here, prepare to move to the country. Our Angkar will welcome you everywhere. From now on, there are no schools, no markets."

Everyone applauded after his speech. While he spoke, we saw soldiers dumping all the school records out of the building and burning them. We felt shocked and hopeless. The big crowd separated and everybody went off to different destinations. I wondered who this "Angkar" was . . . I thought it must be a powerful, high-ranking person in the Khmer Rouge regime. I wanted to see what he looked like.

After I got home, one of my friends from school, Kosal, showed up at our front door in a panic. He looked terrified. My father answered the door, and Kosal spoke to him. "Khmer Rouge soldiers evacuated everyone in my neighborhood, including my family, sir," he said. He kneeled down in front of my father and clasped both hands together. "I want to marry Rina."

My body froze, then I began to sweat. I thought Kosal was out of his mind. I knew what my father was going to do—he would kill me and punch Kosal. My father looked at me and helped Kosal stand up. "Don't worry!" he replied. "Hurry back home and get your mother. We can go to our house in the country together." It took my breath away to hear his kindness. I felt that I owed my father a million things. But I was also curious to know why he was so understanding.

"Thank you very much," Kosal cried. He whispered to me, "Bye Rina! I'll see you later. Don't leave without me." He sent me a thousand hopes with his smile, then he left.

We planned to go back to our house in the country. For the next two days, on the street in front of our house a stream of people walked back and forth. The ones who had no oxcart held their belongings on their head. Small children helped their parents carry chickens and roosters and led the cows. My neighbors, friends, and relatives stopped by to say good-bye with a kind of sadness and disappointment. No one knew where they were going. They couldn't make a plan; only a short-term plan, and sometimes that changed, too.

∾

Suddenly, on April 24, the sound of guns and loud booms exploded everywhere like popcorn, followed by the sound of people screaming like hell. I rushed to the street and saw a group of people heading out of the city as fast as water falling from a pump. I heard someone say, "Go! Go to the countryside quickly! The Americans are going to drop a bomb now! Go! Go!" People ran and ran. Children cried for their parents. Wives looked for husbands. Cows and buffalo cried out, terrified by the guns. Soldiers threatened every house, forcing people at gunpoint to evacuate the city.

My mother and siblings quickly jumped on my uncle's oxcart and he headed for our village, Kompong Rokar. I was horrified because Kosal had just left. I did not want to leave him behind, because we had promised to wait for him. I stood like a statue, my eyes open very wide, and looked for him. My father screamed at me, "Let's go!"

"I'm waiting for Kosal," I said.

"It's too dangerous! Let's go! Hurry! He knows where we live in the country! Go! Go!"

My father pulled my hand tight and we ran, mingling with the other people on the street. Behind us, guns shot. Blood was all over the street and we had to jump over bodies. Some children got lost and no one bothered to take care of them. Elders were also left on the street and cried out for help. After we ran about three miles, I stopped and waited for Kosal for more than two hours. While waiting, I grabbed some books along the road. Everyone else carried food; I carried books. Kosal did not show up. My parents had already gone ahead of me. I started to walk, carrying the books. The more I walked, the heavier the books became. I dropped them one by one about every quarter mile, except one book that Kosal liked very much, *The Last House*. I wondered if I would ever see him again.

CHAPTER 8

The First Blows

AFTER THAT, MY FAMILY LIVED in our house in the country. In April, the temperature in Pursat could get up to 100 degrees, and it was very humid. To the southwest of our house there were no trees, only rice fields, which made the temperature even higher. Sometime a wind blew and eased the temperature down a bit.

My younger siblings were happy because there was no school. They ran and played. My father took care of his animals. I was bored, missed my friends, and felt hopeless waiting for Kosal. I learned that the Khmer Rouge did not like long hair. My mother cut my hair and put the bundle of cut hair on the wall as a keepsake.

Every day, I searched for Kosal by asking the newcomers who passed in front of my house about him. No one had heard anything. I felt guilty for leaving him behind. I thought of all kinds of things that could have happened to him.

On April 26, I saw the Khmer Rouge soldiers bring a full truckload of people who had worked for the Lon Nol government to go "study" at a place called Tol Pra Chrey, fifty kilometers from Pursat, near Tonle Sap Lake. Tol Pra Chrey used to be a stronghold of the Lon Nol government, and the Khmer Rouge soldiers had trouble attacking it.

One afternoon I heard my uncle, a former army officer, saying good-bye to his wife and my grandparents. They cried and hugged each other. A neighbor told my grandmother to tell my uncle to escape because Angkar would certainly kill him as a soldier. This was the last time my grandparents saw their youngest son alive.

A few days later, while standing on the road looking for Kosal, I saw a bulldozer from Tol Pra Chrey drive by. Many flies flew around it. I heard that all soldiers and ex-government employees, including my uncle, had been killed. I was 100 percent certain that I would not survive, because the Khmer Rouge soldiers treated anyone who knew how to read both Khmer and foreign languages as their enemy. I worried about my father, my uncle, and my other relatives, who were soldiers, teachers, nurses, police officers, and students.

We stayed at our house in the country for about four weeks. In the chaos of this time, many parents forced their children to marry. They heard that Angkar was looking for girls to marry the handicapped Khmer Rouge soldiers. New People and Old people did not like each other very much. My parents were worried about me. Like me, they hoped Kosal would show up so they could see my marriage take place.

On May 30, soldiers ordered us to leave our house. They advised us, "All people are equal; no rich, no poor, no big house, no small house." A soldier continued, "All your property—house, land, animals, jewelry—belongs to Angkar." Who is Angkar? I asked myself again. What kind of person is he? Why does he have so much power? Where does he live?

A soldier told my father, "Because you are a teacher, you will stay at the teachers' shelter. Your family will leave everything here. You can take some clothes and one bag of rice." He left before he finished speaking. My mother cried and asked my father, "How will we feed our children?" He comforted her and asked her not to complain.

The next day, June 1, my family moved to a new place, along with twenty other families. The soldiers divided people into groups of twenty to thirty families. Three to five groups formed a commune or *Sa-Hakaor.* The communes were part of a district or *Srok,* which was in turn part of a region or *Tamban.*

Angkar gave us a few square feet of land, enough to make a small hut. We all helped find materials such as bamboo and palm leaves. It took us three days to complete our hut. Angkar would not allow people to have a kitchen at home. Soldiers turned one big house in a village into a main kitchen that could serve 200 to 300 people. Three to five people from a group were assigned to cook. Families were allowed to boil water at home for someone who was sick, but they had to be careful not to add anything else to the pot, such as rice or potatoes. When the soldiers came to someone's hut and checked and found food in the cooking pot, they would arrest the family and accuse them of betraying Angkar. The family could be killed.

Step by step, the new regime moved people to work in the rice fields. Men had to plow the rice fields and take care of the bulls. Women, including widows and older single women, planted rice and did farming. The boys' and girls' teams were considered Angkar's strongest groups. These teams worked on a variety of difficult tasks, such as working at the camp, carrying dirt, harvesting rice, and moving from one place to another as Angkar needed. Children lived at an orphanage and were taken care of by Old People. Children were not allowed to visit their parents. Children belonged to Angkar. They were taught to hate their parents and to kill their own parents when they made mistakes.

My mother looked very tired. She cried most of the time because she was not used to living like this. She was separated from her children, except her baby, and she was worried about my father. One day, a neighbor's son came and told my mother that a soldier had been looking for my father. At the time, my mother was preparing the mosquito net for our family. I saw her standing as she tied the net to the wall. She stood there without moving until my baby brother woke her.

Day by day, my mother looked more depressed. She lost weight and did not sleep at night because she was afraid the soldiers would take my father and kill him, afraid Angkar would take me away from her. She lost her appetite and did not eat. Finally, she did not have enough milk for her baby.

One night I had a dream about eating a guava fruit. In Cambodian belief, this fruit was a symbol of separation. The next day, for the first time Angkar asked my team to work in a rice field far away from my group, about an hour or two away. That day, I felt very strange. I laughed for no reason. I told weird stories to my friends on my team. I wanted to sing a song that I had never heard. While everyone else took a nap during break time, I could not sleep. Our team left the field before sunset. I walked home at around five P.M. My stomach was crawling and growling with hunger. I expected that my mother would be cooking for me.

At our hut, I saw my father carrying my baby brother and doing the cooking. It was unusual to see my father cooking and my mother asleep on the bamboo bed, with a striped blanket covering her body.

I was unhappy because I had expected the food to be ready. I let my father take care of my brother and I started to cook. As soon as I finished cooking, I heard my mother call my father. I was glad to hear her voice. I wanted to impress her with the wonderful job of cooking I did. Suddenly, her last sentence surprised and woke me up. "Honey! Where are our children, please bring them in. I want to give them my last word." As soon as she said that, all my brothers and sisters, who were playing around the hut, gathered around her quickly.

Crying, the children bent down to my mother and listened expectantly. First she addressed my father. "Honey! We've been married for almost twenty years. We have a wonderful marriage. You are a good husband and a good father. Thank you for sharing your life with me. Now it is time for you to raise our children without me."

"Don't say such things, honey, you must stay with us for the sake of the children," my father interrupted her. But she did not reply to my father; instead, she addressed each one of us. "Rina! Without me here, you will take my place. You are the caretaker of your brothers and sisters and your father. Rinal! As a boy, you will help your father around the house and protect your sisters. All the younger children, you should listen and follow your older sister and brother's advice."

All of us, including the baby, were crying so much that we attracted the neighbors' attention. A big crowd of neighbors came and filled the hut. The line of people extended outside the hut. They were shocked to see my mother in this serious condition. My mother talked to the neighbors while nursing her baby. "Please, when Angkar evacuates our group, bring my children along with you." Everyone tried to support her, but they could do nothing to help with her condition.

My father was the family doctor. He was so frustrated because the market was closed, and our money was useless. How was he going to find medicine for my mother? Only gold could be exchanged for medicine. Who would be willing to do this? How could a doctor save his patient's life without medication?

He paced back and forth. He did not know what to do. One of our neighbors suggested that my father call on my mother's mother, who lived in the next village, for help. My father seemed to wake up from a dream. He said, "Thank you for your suggestion. I've never experienced anything like this. I'm lost." Then he asked my brother Rinal to go get my grandmother. I was worried about Rinal's safety because it was getting dark and he had to make a shortcut across the rice field, which was very muddy.

I thought of a million things that could happen to my mother and my family. The elders asked me to make food for my siblings to eat. Neighbors came by to see my mother. They looked at her with sadness and hopelessness. They had nothing to offer to help support my family. After a while, one by one the neighbors left so we would have room for the next visitor. My mother was still nursing the baby. One neighbor who just had a baby offered to nurse our baby, but my mother refused.

My grandmother arrived with my brother. They looked awful—they had walked with bare feet and mud covered their faces. My grandmother went straight in to see her daughter. After observing her, she cried out and recommended that my father invite Achar, the shaman, to come. "She is seriously ill. You must bring Achar—the sooner the better. Hurry! Hurry!" As soon as my father left to go for Achar, the neighbors went home. All my siblings cried and hovered around my mother until they fell asleep with dry tear stains on their faces.

My mother was getting worse and worse. My grandmother knew very well that my mother was going to die soon. But she did not tell me the truth. She asked me to stay close to my mother. Sometimes my mother was confused and she hallucinated, which gave my grandmother a chance to pull the baby away from her. She held the baby and comforted him to sleep as she wept about the bond between her and my mother. She described memories from the time my mother was a child up until she married my father. My mother was her beloved daughter who had sacrificed everything for her. They had never lived apart for more than three months. They built their houses next to each other. They got along very well. They always consulted each other, even with a simple problem.

While my grandmother talked about her memories, suddenly my mother had a serious convulsion that wracked her body. She quickly sat up straight, grabbed my hands, and asked for water. I saw her face turn into a white cloth and her eyeballs roll up to the roof. She looked like a ghost in the movies. But this was real. My grandmother grabbed the baby and jumped outside the hut. I felt scared too, but I thought, she is my mother. No matter what, I have to be with her, to take care of her. After giving my mother a cup of water, I laid her down to sleep.

Outside, the sky was full of black clouds and there were no

stars that I could see. Thunder followed the piercing lightning and growled threateningly to let me know that he controlled the universe and I was powerless. It started to sprinkle and a chilly gust of air blew fiercely. The sound of thunder, the cold wind, the rain, and the darkness mixed into a haunted music that screamed into my ears to trap my soul and push my body over the cliff of despair. An owl perched on the roof and cried out to claim my mother's soul.

I pulled my grandmother and the baby inside the hut to avoid getting wet and comforted her that everything was fine. She agreed to come in and continued to talk about her journey with my mother. I went back to my mother and massaged her. Her feet felt strange. They seemed cool and less sensitive. She continued to have hallucinations, nightmares, and confusion, and her voice changed constantly. Sometimes it was hard to understand her. I waited for my father. He had to walk a long way to Achar's house in the dark, in the storm and thunder. I knew he loved my mother so much that nothing would stop him.

Around ten o'clock that night, my father arrived, accompanied by Achar. My father rushed to my mother to see if she had made any progress. I was relieved to have him back. After diagnosing my mother, Achar informed us that she was going to die in half an hour. This shocked my father. He sat by Achar and stared at my mother and held her hands. Without medication, my father could not save her life. Achar asked for our support to talk to my mother and have her repeat the Buddha's words after him.

He believed that the Buddha's words would help her find a way to heaven. *Chan Heang. Preak pout preak thor . . . preak sang.* "Repeat it, my lovely daughter," my grandmother screamed so she could hear these important words. Everyone forced her to repeat the words. I felt her feet getting stiff and becoming colder and colder. I kept massaging her from her toes to her feet, to her knees, and then up to her thighs. I realized that I was going to lose my mother soon. Her voice changed and sounded completely different until the words *Preak pout preak thor* and *Preak sang* faded away and could not be understood. Finally, we heard only breath pumping out. We listened to this sound for a couple of minutes until the Achar burned incense and talked to her soul and prayed. The voice sounded lower and lower until it was completely gone. My mother was pronounced dead at ten P.M. on June 15, 1975. She was thirty-seven years old.

As soon as Achar stopped speaking, I screamed and ran to wake up my siblings. "My dear brothers and sisters, our mother has said good-bye to us! Wake up, wake up! She is dead, we have lost our beloved mother! She's leaving us." My brothers and sisters woke up to see our mother's dead body and our small hut full of horrible voices of grief, sadness, and sorrow. I was so angry that I ran outside and screamed for help. I swore at Angkar, who killed my mother by letting her die without medicine to cure her illness. A former student of my father grabbed me back inside and put his hand over my mouth to stop me from assaulting Angkar.

Early the next morning, the bell was rung for the death of my mother. This sound would spread the bad news all over my village and other nearby villages. Word of mouth passed very quickly. Later, people who knew my mother came to offer their condolences, to say that they could hardly take it and were very sorry, and to share our sorrow. My grandfather arrived shortly after my grandmother asked her neighbor to send him the news. He hugged my mother's body, then removed the white cloth to see her face. He stared at her for a long time, his face full of tears. I knew that my mother was his favorite daughter. I had not seen him cry at all when my uncle was killed recently. Only his sad face showed that he thought about him.

My father felt lost and confused. My grandparents and my father decided to arrange a cremation at the temple around noon, cutting short the ceremony to avoid trouble with the Communist rulers, who did not allow people to follow this old tradition anymore.

Around noon, people from the village helped carry my

mother's coffin, put it in a wheel cart, and pushed it to the temple. While they were pushing the cart, I walked alongside it and looked through a small hole in the coffin. I saw part of my mother's deadly pale face. My heart felt like someone had stabbed a knife in it, twisted it around, and left it there. Then I walked behind the cart, which was moving slowly, carrying her unwakeable body, a body that no longer produced milk to nourish and nurture my siblings, a body that I wanted to be with eternally, a body that gave me safety and security. Now this body had left me without saying good-bye, without telling me where she was going, without leaving me any clue so I could find her.

My father comforted me, "My dear, she passed away, she does not suffer like us. We are left behind, we don't know what will happen to us, please calm down." It made me feel better for a little while, and I paid attention to my baby brother and other siblings. The cremation took place outside the temple. Achar and some other people prepared to cremate my mother. They set up a big pile of wood on a rectangular block of cement where they would put my mother's body. They lifted her coffin out of the cart and put it on top of the wood. Everyone started to cry again. The men poured gasoline into the coffin and dropped matches into it. A long flame burst up and smoke filled the sky, taking my mother's soul away from us—from this world, to heaven, leaving us behind to live in hell. The red flame and black smoke twisted, twirled, and spread over half the village to say a last good-bye to all the villagers who stood silently, burdened with the loss of my mother. They asked questions like, "Why does a good person like her have to die first?"

Suddenly I heard a voice crying from a distance, getting closer and closer. "Cher [Sister]! Why are you are leaving us, I'm sorry I'm late." Then my uncle came and comforted all my brothers and sisters.

Around three P.M., Achar asked people to bring water to pour on the fire so my family would have a chance to pick up her bones and keep them at the temple, following our tradition.

That night, my grandparents stayed with us to help with the baby. The baby cried all night long for milk. The adults were up all night long, looking at each other hopelessly. We thought about a cow, but there was no cow that we could milk. We thought about asking someone who was breastfeeding, but she would want to save the milk for her own baby. The only solution was to cook rice soup for him, but he was so young to eat soup.

It was very difficult for me, my father, and the other children to face reality. The youngest children kept asking me about my mother because they had waited for her for a long time and she never returned. I didn't know how to answer their questions. She was gone forever and would not come back to us. At lunch and supper, we missed her badly. We used to see her in a circle, feeding us with good food. She told jokes and funny stories and made us laugh constantly until the stern, quiet look in my father's eyes made us fall silent. Yet I felt that she was still with us, cooking, cleaning, talking, and laughing. I could hear her voice inside the hut. I had never felt pain like this before. It was a sharp pain, a suffering I could not find words to describe.

My father and I felt that we could not take care of the baby, because we had no experience, especially raising a baby without milk. We asked my grandmother to care for him. According to the Communist rule, however, she could not do that because we lived in different groups. So I became a young mother at age seventeen, caring for the baby and my eight other siblings. In addition, I had to do work such as cutting wheat to make fertilizer. I was very exhausted because I could not sleep at night. I did not want to wake up my father for help because he also worked so hard. I let him have a good night's sleep.

The baby cried day and night for breast milk. He cried until his mouth was dry and his tears stopped falling. He started to lose weight and was unable to eat rice soup. He threw up every time the soup reached his stomach. My eighth sister, who was just about eighteen months old, was also sick. I had to take care of both of them. My father worked hard to find sugar for the baby by walking from one village to another. He begged people for sugar to save his baby's life. If he was lucky, he got a can of sweetened milk, which allowed the baby to live and to smile for a couple of days. When the milk was gone, he got sick again.

✺

Once in a while my grandmother came to visit my family, but not for long because she had to get back to work. When I caught a cold, I asked my grandmother to take care of my eighteen-month-old sister. I felt that I could not take care of both her and the baby. She agreed to help, which gave me a little break.

Two months passed very slowly. With my short hair and my sleeplessness and dark eyes, I looked like an old grandmother. My baby brother was getting sicker and sicker. Sometimes I could not bring him to work with me. I put him in the hammock so he could sleep better. One afternoon while I worked, I heard a strange cry from the baby in the hammock. I ran to pick him up. A bloody bubble popped out of his nose. I screamed for help. The neighbor next door came but did not say anything. She shook her head and cried. I knew that my brother was not going to live. He did not cry very much anymore; most of the time he slept.

In the evening after supper, I told my father about the baby. We looked at each other and he decided to ask my grandmother to come again. At midnight, she woke up my father and me and told us about her dream. She said that she saw my mother standing near the baby, and my mother told her that she had come to take the baby. She complained that no one knew how to take care of her baby. We looked at the baby for a while, and then we fell asleep. I heard the baby making sounds like he was snoring. Blood came out his nose. At five in the morning on August 18, the baby died. My father buried him next to my mother's ashes.

Our family home, built in 1958 in Kompong Rokar

CHAPTER 9

The End Of Our House

AT THE END OF 1975, my work team was sent to work at a camp someplace else. I was assigned to be a village guard to check and verify the papers of people who traveled from one village to another. They had to have a letter authorizing their travel. I had a chance to meet all kinds of people, Old and New—except Kosal.

One day, while standing near a tamarind tree, I noticed a cloud in the middle of a sunny sky. There was no air moving. It was very calm and quiet. I ducked my head to protect it from the rain. Suddenly, a flash of lightning struck about 600 yards from where I stood. I didn't know what had happened, but I heard thunder and my body fell to the ground face down. No one else was around. I tried to get up but I couldn't. It seemed like my body had lost some kind of special energy. My eyes were open, very alert, and my nose was breathing. An old man who lived nearby came outside after hearing an awful sound. He found my motionless body. He jumped back and forth over me, then lay me on my back, put his hand on my head, recited some words, and blew three times in my face. I was able to sit up and I asked him what was going on. He told me that lightning struck the palm tree. He pointed to the tree, which was burning at the top.

"There are two kinds of lightning that hit the ground," he explained. "One produces fire, as you see, and the other produces water. You are very lucky that the lightning did not strike straight in your direction, otherwise you would not have survived."

I thanked the old man for saving my life. I stood with my body trembling and watched the palm tree in flames. I could not believe my own eyes that lightning could burn a green tree like paper.

After my baby brother died, Angkar separated my family. They sent my father with the men's team to pioneer a farm far away from my group. My sister and I were sent with the girl's team to dig a dam near National Route 5. My brother went with his boy's team to destroy the big houses in Ken Dieng. Angkar wanted everyone to live equally, so big houses were torn down or made the same size as the smaller houses. The rest of my siblings stayed at the orphanage.

❧

In September 1976, my team was called by Angkar to work in a rice field near my home village. I was happy because I would get a chance to see my family home, which I had not seen since the Communist soldiers evacuated my family. I was so anxious to see how my house looked.

September was the rainy season. All the girls on the team, including me, walked in the rain and the darkness to my village. In the pouring rain, we walked with soaking wet clothes. I was chilled. I was starved for food and very sleepy. I walked with my eyes closed and held my friend's hand.

I was woken up when I heard my team leader yell, "Let's stay in the house ahead." When we reached the house, I slept in my wet clothes. Early the next morning, I was the only one awake. I looked at the walls of the house, the roof, the windows, the doors. . . . "Ah! This is my house!" I murmured. It had been two years since Angkar kicked my family off our property. I had spent seventeen years in this house. Now my lovely home had become a hall that could hold 150 persons.

Unexpected luck! I tried to calm down and started looking

around. The walls were full of holes, punched in by axes. The furniture was missing. My bed was torn apart. Mattresses had been cut open and feathers blew all around the room. I walked to the kitchen where my mother used to cook, but it didn't smell of good spicy food anymore. As I entered, I felt my mother there, chuckling and cutting the pork bones as hard as the musician beats the drum. It seemed as if I was walking toward her, but she wasn't there. Only my feelings, my memories, bound me to my mother. In the kitchen, I remembered, I used to feel safe and protected by my mother.

On the way to the kitchen door I saw a broken table and chairs. A small handmade jar, a gift from my grandmother for my parents' wedding, was broken in two, with a little dirty water in it. Plates, forks, spoons, and chopsticks were destroyed and splayed on the floor in many directions. Wandering around, crossing the stairway to the balcony, where I used to play with my younger brothers and sisters, I recognized an old blanket that I used when I slept with my mother. I remembered how comfortable I was at that time.

As I glanced to the right, I found a fragmented picture of my parents. I picked it up and held it to my chest. Looking at the picture, I saw a note written on it: "King of the village." This was the clue they had to empty my family out of the house! I carried the picture to the balcony. My baby brother's hammock was there, torn apart. The little toy bird that hung over his head and used to sing a beautiful song to him was missing its head. Its broken wing lay on the other side of the room.

I sat down, closed my eyes, and used my imagination to hear my siblings—their joy, their laughter, their screams, and their quiet moments when they listened to the ghost stories my grandfather told. I felt very exhausted. I had not had enough food to eat the night before. I fell down on the floor and cried, keeping an eye on the corner of the balcony. Seeing my mother's torn old shoes, I crept over to pick them up. Suddenly, a foot with a black Khmer Rouge sandal stepped on my hand and a mean loud voice said, "You're the owner of this house?"

"No, my dear friend," I replied.

"Why are you holding that picture to your chest?" he continued with grinning teeth and a dirty look.

"No, my dear friend . . . I tried to take the frame off and burn it to cook for our team," I answered. He seemed to find this a reasonable answer. "Wake up, it's time to go to work," he yelled to everybody. He blew his whistle. I felt so tired. I did not want to go to work but I had to, otherwise my food ration would be cut off.

Outside, it was still raining. My clothes were not dry yet and they smelled bad. Everyone went to the rice fields behind my house. My mind stayed behind with my mother's old shoes, my old blanket, and everything in my house. Suddenly I saw my cows, the two blacks and the two browns. Angkar was using them to plow the field. My lovely best friends were so skinny. They were working hard liked me. All four cows stopped in front of me. They wanted to tell me that they missed me very much. The plowers looked puzzled when they saw that the cows were not walking. I asked my browns quietly, "Where are your other twenty-five relatives?" Tears fell from their eyes and I knew that they still recognized me. The plowers beat them and then we were separated.

∾

I put my feet into the deep mud and, taking small pieces of rice plants, one by one I pushed them into the mud with my thumb. At break time, my eyes turned to my friends, Browns and Blacks, and to my house. I memorized every aspect as I looked around. Then I heard the soldiers call my name. As I walked toward them, I was thinking about my death. They knew I was the owner of the house. I was afraid to look at the soldiers' faces. They asked me to pass a message to the team to move to another place nearby. I felt a little better, but I was disappointed because I wanted to stay at my house for another couple of days.

∾

It was raining, with lightning and thunder. My tears fell hard and mixed with the rain when I had to leave my house. I thought this would be the last time I would see it.

My team worked at different places in the area. One day, I told my leader that I was sick. The truth was that I wanted to see my house one last time before my team moved the next morning. I agreed to stay by myself without food, just for the chance to say good-bye.

I walked toward my house. As I got close, I heard "Pong! Pang! Pong! Pang!" It sounded like someone doing construction work. I saw a group of soldiers on the road ahead of me with materials loaded on an oxcart. I moved away from them and hid in the bushes nearby. Through the small branches and leaves, I could see the soldiers' activities clearly. A tall, dark-skinned man with a green and white kramar on his head, who looked like a marijuana addict, attached long ropes to the wall of my house. A short, light-skinned man wearing a cap went into my house; then a couple of giant men appeared on the roof with axes and hammers.

"Oh my god! Angkar has condemned my lovely house." I clapped my hand over my mouth to silence my voice. My heart pounded. I was sweating. My body trembled. My eyes did not blink. I was afraid to miss a moment of the destruction of my house.

The walls began to fall down; the clay tiles on the roof were broken piece by piece. The stairs were pushed out of the house. Two men with hammers smashed the kitchen walls. A tall, muscular man with a long gun on his shoulder dumped the broken chairs and tables into the front yard. Three men pushed the floor away.

In just a couple of hours, the house where my family and I

had lived in peace and happiness was completely destroyed. One soldier ordered another to cut the coconut and orange trees down. I was very angry. I remembered how my father had worked so hard to take care of those trees. Under the orange trees was a good place for my brothers and sisters to play. We used to hang the hammock between two trees and pretend to sleep when my father grounded us.

I felt heat spread from my body to my face. I sweated like I was taking a shower. I almost did something to protect my property—and let them kill me. I wanted to die with my house. But I thought about the eight brothers and sisters I would leave behind. I knew they would not live safely if I did that.

My house and all the fruit trees—mango, coconut, and orange—were destroyed before sunset on my birthday, September 10. It was a painful loss and it hurt, but I will never forget every moment of happiness I had with my family in that beautiful home.

CHAPTER 10

One Can Of Rice

By the fall of 1976, starvation was widespread across the country. The main kitchen in our commune received just five cans of rice for 200 people. Many people were suffering from malnutrition, malaria, fever, cholera, diarrhea, and dysentery. There was no medicine to help.

Especially hard hit were those who had been evacuated from Phnom Penh. They were city people who didn't know a thing about living as a peasant. Some hardly knew the difference between a rice plant and wheat. They had a difficult time adjusting.

Angkar tortured and executed teachers, soldiers, students, and ex-government workers. Some ex-government workers managed to hide their profession from the soldiers, but they could not run away from starvation.

Everyone stole and lied in order to survive. New jails opened everywhere. Travel restrictions were strictly enforced, and soldiers guarded each commune.

I saw dead bodies everywhere. The smell was awful. In every village, there were fewer and fewer people on the street, in the houses, and at work. People who were in the final stages of starvation did not care if the soldiers killed them. The only thing they wanted before they stopped breathing was to eat some rice. People crawled to the jungle to look for wild potatoes and edible trees. They died halfway there with their eyes open. The ants made nests in their eyes and ears. Flies swarmed around their mouths. A couple of days later, crows and wolves finished off the corpses.

I continued to lose weight. I was so skinny that I could count all the bones in my body. My eyes were sunk deep into my face. My chest was completely flat, the skin stretched tightly across my ribs. My tailbone hurt when I lay down to sleep on the cement floor. Every time I moved my body, I felt a sharp pain like a rough rock rolling around inside me. My knees were as big as my head, and my arm and leg bones were long as sticks. I could see the small veins like worms under my skin. My skin was as parched as a rice field that had had no rain for months.

The moment my eyes opened in the morning, I was hungry. I saw and smelled and daydreamed food. I ate anything I could find, from leaves to bugs or other creatures. I cried for food until there were no tears. I screamed for food until I couldn't swallow. I asked myself if it was time for me to leave this world. Would I die of starvation or of torture? My only wish was to end my life, so I would no longer have to work like an animal.

∾

In spite of my starvation, I was forced to work in the rice fields. If I refused, my meager food ration was cut off. At five o'clock each morning, the soldiers whistled to wake up the group. Anyone who was sick and unable to get up was beaten with a long stick or gun.

While I was planting rice one day, I asked my group leader for permission to rest. She said no. I was forced to keep working. I felt dizzy. My ears were ringing. My legs were weak from standing for so long in the mud. Pulling my legs out of the mud was the most difficult thing in the world. Rain fell harder and harder. Chilled, my body shook.

My eyes couldn't see. My ears couldn't hear. My body had nothing to hang onto. I felt dizzy and collapsed into the mud . . . .

I found myself lying near a tree on the dike. My body was very hot, as though I had just come from a steam room. My head was heavy, like I was wearing a helmet. I was very thirsty. I could not get up. I didn't see anyone around. I crawled like a turtle toward the water in the rice paddy. I wished that a cobra would bite me, so my suffering would end.

Instead of returning to the girl's team, I decided to go see my father before I died. He lived about five kilometers from where I was. I missed him so much, especially since I was sick. He had always taken good care of me. I wanted to die in his arms.

I trudged across the rice field. I sat down every ten yards to rest. Out of nowhere I heard a child cry for help. I stood up and peeked. I saw a skinny young boy wearing ragged gray shorts and no shirt. He was being hit by a soldier. I sat back down and crawled into the rice paddy to hide. The soldier and the boy walked past me. The poor little boy's face was full of tears. An open wound on his right hand was bleeding.

After the soldier was gone, I continued to walk. I caught some crabs along the dike for my father. I saw two bulls coming toward the rice paddy. I grabbed their leads and pulled them away. If the soldiers caught the bulls eating rice, they would kill the person who was taking care of them. About ten yards later, I heard a groaning sound. I walked toward the voice. It was my father. He had fallen in the mud and could not get up. I was so sad to see my father in that helpless situation, but I could find no words to share with him. Instead, my tears showed him my love and concern. He stared dimly at me with pale eyes. His bony face showed his white teeth as he tried to smile at me. His clothes were dirty, and thick mud covered his body. He tried to get up, but he couldn't.

I started to pull his arms and legs out of the mud, but I was also weak. I fell on him, and we both landed flat on our faces. Luckily, I was still holding the bulls' lines. The bulls pulled on the line and helped us get out of the mud. I used my kramar and some water to clean off my father. We walked toward his hut with the two bulls, stopping many times along the way. At my father's hut, I fixed some crab soup for him. We looked at each other over an oil lamp. For a moment, it felt just like old times.

I decided to stay overnight with my father. I didn't care if the soldiers found me and killed me, as long as I had this moment with my father. I preferred to die in his arms. Late that evening, my brother Ra and sister Sokna sneaked out of the orphanage to join us too. We all looked at each other closely—our bodies were so different that we barely recognized each other.

Lying on the hard floor next to me, my father told me that he had seen my fiancé, Kosal, driving an oxcart carrying rice. Kosal worked as a ricekeeper not far from my commune.

"I wanted to ask him for some rice, but I couldn't," my father said. "There were a couple of soldiers escorting him. I didn't want him to get in trouble. He is young and can live longer than I." As he talked, my father started to fall asleep. He was exhausted.

In the dim light of the fish-oil lamp, I looked at him with a heavy heart. I whispered into his ear about some people who had successfully escaped to Thailand. He didn't want to hear about it. He discouraged me from trying to escape. "Daughter! If you go, you can't come back, you know that. They will kill you." He shook his head very slowly. Then he switched the subject back to Kosal. Kosal was in charge of the rice warehouse, my father said, and he looked very healthy. I could read between the lines of what my father said about Kosal. It was a clue about his own hunger. My father was the only one I had left. My obligation was to find rice for him. My father had taken care of me when I was sick. Now I had an opportunity to show him respect by asking Kosal for rice.

I did not sleep that night. I thought about how to find Kosal. I touched my bony face and head. I looked like an ugly old grandma with wrinkled skin and hard straw hair that hadn't been shampooed or combed for decades. I did not want Kosal to see me like this. Would he still recognize me and accept me? Two years of separation seemed too long. I never thought about him anymore. I had assumed that Kosal was dead. But sometimes my memory still called forth his name, his kindness, his caresses, and his words. One mysterious question haunted me—what had happened to him? Why didn't he come back to me? I was anxious to see him and ask him my questions.

At 5:00 the next morning, while my father and siblings were still asleep, I left to go look for Kosal and ask him for rice for my father. I walked across the rice field instead of on the road, because I didn't have a permission letter to travel. I had no energy to walk, but the hope of bringing rice to my father gave me strength. By the time the sun was over my head, I was tired. I rested under a palm tree. Palm juice dropped onto my hand and I licked it. It was sweet and tasty. After having about ten drops of palm juice, I had the energy to continue my journey. I crossed a small dam. After three or four steps, suddenly my feet sank deeply into the mud. My weak legs fell deeper and deeper, and I feared getting caught by soldiers.

I wanted to scream for help but I couldn't. There was nothing around me except some tall wild rice plants. I reached toward a bundle of wild rice and used it to pull my body from the mud. I tried once, again, and finally wrench myself out of the mud. I sat quietly to calm down. My heart was pounding. My hands and legs were shaking. My ears were ringing. I thought my breath would give out.

After resting a little while, I started walking again and saw the roof of the main kitchen rising above Kosal's village. I arrived around sunset. In the middle of the village, by the light of a torch, I saw a young woman with an unpleasant face dividing rice among members of the village. She was dressed in the black Khmer Rouge uniform, with a kramar tied around her head. As I headed toward the kitchen to ask for information, I stepped on a dead palm leaf. The loud crackle attracted the woman's attention. Two men ran toward the sound and found me. They brought me to the lady in the black uniform.

"Ha! Thief girl . . . look at you, it's not even dark yet, and you're already coming to steal." She pointed a finger in my face.

"No! No! I am not a thief," I protested quickly.

"You've stolen our vegetables many times. I've finally caught you! Take her to the soldiers' station. I don't want to hear a word from her," she added.

"Please! Let me explain." I knelt down and begged her while I looked at the rice on the table and swallowed, my mouth empty.

I never got a chance to explain. The two men quickly tied my hands behind my back. They pushed me forward with a long stick and pulled my hair in different directions. It was very dark. There was no moon in the sky, only a little starlight. I reproached myself that I could have avoided this trouble. The two men dropped me off at the soldiers' station and left.

The soldiers there put me in a jail that looked like a metal cage. In the cage next to mine, I heard a girl cry out, complaining of a sharp pain. I smelled blood. Mosquitoes were biting the other inmates and me. I felt sorry for the inmates whose legs and hands were in chains. The girl's groans disrupted my sleep. I had heard that exact sound somewhere before, but I could not remember where. I wanted to comfort her.

"What is the matter, friend?" I whispered.

"Soldiers. . . accused . . . my . . . my . . . husband of being one of Lon Nol's soldiers," she tried to explain in a weak voice. "My husband ran away. . ." She coughed. "When . . . they asked me about him. . . . I don't know . . . then the soldiers beat me up. . . . until I lost my baby . . . it is very painful . . . the blood runs like water . . . it hurts. . ."

"Wait a minute," I interrupted her. "I recognize your voice—you must be Bunny."

"And . . . and . . . you're Rina!" she murmured. "I am glad to see you before my life ends."

During that unforgettable night, we talked and talked for hours before we finally fell sleep. In the morning, when I woke up, the conversation from the night before seemed like a dream. In the next cage, my friend Bunny lay in her blood. The pain was bad. Again, I comforted her. We had a chance to look at each other face to face, but our conversation was interrupted by the mean voice of a woman soldier. In her hand the soldier held a bowl of rice soup for my friend. But instead of giving it to her, that witch poured it on Bunny's head. The soup dripped through her hair and fell down to her lap. She tried to reach it with her tongue, licking every drop she could. The witch soldier laughed, making fun of her. Then I saw Bunny's body shake. Her mouth opened and her eyes stared at me. She died calling my name. Two soldiers came to remove her body, and I cried without tears.

∾

An hour later, a soldier took me to another room, a small, dark place full of plastic bags, ropes, wires, and long sticks. The stench of blood filled the room. After seeing what was in the room, I didn't think I'd have a chance to see my father, who was waiting for rice. Two men came with guns. I closed my eyes and prayed. I knew they were going to hurt me. When I opened my eyes, I recognized one of the soldiers. Five foot eleven inches tall, with light skin, he had a dimple on his right cheek. He was dressed in a black Khmer Rouge soldier's uniform with a blue (his favorite color) kramar tied around his waist. It was Kosal. He looked the same as when I had last seen him, two years ago. But why would he carry a gun? He was considered one of the New People. I did not understand. While I tried to sort these things out, his partner picked up a couple of plastic bags and left. I looked straight into Kosal's eyes and called his name. He was surprised when he heard his name spoken clearly.

"It's Rina," I added.

He gave me a weird look. "Rina!" He blew my name out of his mouth. "What happened to you?" He quickly untied my hands.

"Dad is sick, and he told me that you live in this village. I came to see you to ask for rice for him," I said. I continued, "What happened to you? I waited and waited for you but you never came to find me."

"After I left you, my whole village was evacuated," Kosal began. "I was separated from my mother. When I returned to your house, you and your family were gone. I found a three-year-old boy, one of the Old People, who had lost his mother. I helped him find his mother, and in return, she offered to marry her oldest daughter to me. She is the one who sent you over here," he explained. "I am sorry, very sorry, Rina!"

"And. . I . . I . . .worried about you . . . thought about you . . . but . . ." I sobbed and could not finish the sentence.

The other soldier came back. Kosal told his colleague that I was innocent. Then he gave me a can of rice for my father and a permission letter to go back to my commune. My heart would always be with him, but I promised him I would not bother him anymore. He was married. I wanted him to live peacefully with his wife.

In the afternoon, I arrived at my father's hut, full of joy because I had a can of rice for him. The rice that could satisfy his hunger. The rice that he dreamed about every second. The rice that he was dying to have. I felt strongly that this was the best gift I would ever give him.

At the front door of the hut, I saw my sister crying. I asked her where our father was.

"I called him, but he doesn't answer. Ra went to look for you and I don't know why Father is sleeping so long today," she said.

My body started trembling, the same symptom I usually had. Terrible thoughts spun in my head. I did not want to face the same feelings I had with my mother a year ago. I rushed into the hut and pushed aside the palm rag that divided the room. It was dark except for a ray of sunlight shining through the palm-leaf wall. My father lay on the floor where I had slept next to him. He was dressed in a dark gray, short-sleeved shirt, with his red and white kramar wrapped around his neck to protect him from the cold. One of his hands was on the floor and the other rested across his chest. His eyes were half open, and one clear fresh tear had dropped onto his bony face below his right eye. I tiptoed toward him, carrying the can of rice in my hands, ready to give it to him.

"Dad! Dad!" My voice got louder and louder. Since he did not answer my call, I started to shake him. His hands and legs were stiff and cold. Only his chest still felt warm.

I started to scream and shake his body roughly.

"Dad! Here is some rice. Wake up, Daddy! I've brought you rice! Rice . . . rice . . . rice that will fill your empty stomach, so you can live longer for me . . . for your children . . . for your last words that I wait to hear from you, to share your last moment with me. . . . Why can't you wait for me, Dad! Why? Why? Here is the rice that I worked so hard to get, just for you." I sobbed, looking at the can of rice and my father's body in front of me. "When I was sick, you saved my life. You took care of me, fed me, worked hard for me, looked for every possible way to treat me . . . but when you are sick and hungry . . . I can't even give you this small thing, just one can of rice, Dad! Dad!"

I fell onto his chest and sobbed. My tears mixed with his one teardrop to share the pain and suffering of this last moment. I hugged his body, my throat swollen tight. I closed his eyes and wiped the tear from his face so he would not carry this suffering to his next life. I knelt down and put the can of rice in his shirt pocket so his soul would not starve to death. My sister and I apologized to him for any mistakes we had made. We asked his spirit to find a better place to rest so he would not suffer as he had in this life.

I cried out loud, loud enough to let the world feel my pain and suffering. I did not care if the Communist soldiers killed me. I was out of control.

I cleaned his body with water and wrapped my kramar around him. My sister and brother and I carried him outside. We dug a hole in the ground and started to bury him near his hut. A neighbor came and told me not to bury him so close to the hut, but he would not help me.

I cried out loud again, upset that I had to go through this. My cry caught the attention of the *Ka-Nak-Sa-Hak-Koar,* the Villager in Charge, who rode his bike over from the main kitchen. Seeing that my brother and sister and I had to bury my father by ourselves, he comforted me and ordered some people in the camp to make a coffin for my father.

Volunteers carried my father's body across a rice field. I walked behind them. Four people carried the coffin, which rested on two long wooden sticks on their shoulders. It was the same procedure that we had used for my mother a year ago. We found a place in the rice field, surrounded by palm trees and small bushes. There were many new tombs from recent burials. The volunteers dug the grave. I thanked them for all their help.

My father had a place to rest. We bowed our heads and saluted him good-bye. On December 25, 1976, my father died at age forty-three.

December was monsoon season. The day my father passed away, a chilly wind blew through the rice paddies, making a soft, sad music. I held green rice grains fresh from the rice paddy in my hand and looked at my father's burial place. My tears fell as quickly as pouring rain. I thought about how hard my father had worked without food, on rainy days, in hot and cold weather, or in spite of sickness, to produce this rice crop. But God did not let him wait to harvest this precious grain so he could live another year.

I spoke to my father. "Last night, you slept in the hut; you were a human being. Today your body is unwanted; it is called a 'corpse.' They lowered your body into the ground, which is dirty and full of worms and other insects. Tonight, you sleep in a scary, unknown place, a place without your children, a rectangle in the earth that is all you have for a home.

"At first you may be scared in your new home, but later on you will be happy because this place is peaceful. No soldiers will force you to work, no group leader will yell at you, and no Angkar will threaten you. You'll have no worries, no cows to take care of. You are free. I hope your soul joins Mother. If you find her, tell her how miserable I am living without her. Please ask her to come and protect me.

"When Mother passed away, you and I began to build a very close relationship. I had just started to understand you, to appreciate your greatness as a father. The night I slept near you was my time to say good-bye, and a moment I cannot forget. I will carry this with me forever."

༄

I went back to my father's hut to gather some of his belongings. My brother, sister, and I looked at his place for the last time. Then we began walking toward my grandparents' village to share the sad news with them.

The sun set behind a line of trees alongside the rice paddy, the red rays of the sun sinking slowly into the earth as usual. As we walked out of Father's hut, we were burdened with grief and emptiness, but our minds remained with him. Good-bye Father! I know you are watching us. May your soul be with us forever.

CHAPTER II

Hunger

MY SISTER MOUCH, BROTHER RA, and I walked across the rice field and reached my grandparents' commune at dark. At my grandparents' hut, dropped everything we were carrying and we lay down on the bamboo bed without saying a word. My youngest sister, Soksaroeun, crawled toward me and pointed to my grandparents, who were also very sick. They were lying on another bed, covered with a blanket. My little sister did not know that her father had died. Even though I told her, it didn't make sense to her.

My youngest sister was three years old. Malnourished, she weighed only about twenty pounds. She could not walk or talk. But she could move very fast, and she was wise and alert when she saw soldiers or an unfamiliar face. She understood when people talked. She knew the secret places where my grandmother hid food, such as the small broken jar near a tree in front of the hut. The jar was half filled with water. This was not regular water—it was a salt and water solution. My grandmother fooled soldiers and strangers into thinking it was just dirty water. Under her bamboo bed, there were stocks of cooked rice, dry rice, and dried fish. Angkar would not allow people to have a kitchen at home. No one was allowed to cook except to boil water. Every time my grandmother boiled water, my youngest sister knew there would be an additional ration of rice for her.

My little sister crawled and pointed out some rice soup my

grandmother had not eaten. My grandmother's commune was better off than my commune. They still had adequate food to survive. But, like everyone else, they had no medicine. Diarrhea and dysentery were common. My grandfather was dehydrated from diarrhea and my grandmother had dysentery. She asked me what happened to my father. But she could not offer suggestions or help as she used to do. She sent me to the clinic to ask for medicine. Luckily, I was able to get some Western medicine and a can of sweetened condensed milk by begging the *Yothea* at the nearby hospital. The milk reminded me of my father, and my tears poured out. The medicine saved my grandparents' lives.

After my father's death, I lost all hope for the future. I felt numb. My life made no sense. I was mentally exhausted. Every time I walked across the village, I heard my parents' voices, remembering the way they chatted with neighbors or called my name when they couldn't find me. I thought of their mannerisms, their houses, their animals . . . Every time I breathed, a sharp pain shot through my chest. I rarely talked or made conversation. My ears were blocked from everything. Only my eyes and nose still functioned. The eyes that stayed open almost twenty-four hours a day because they were afraid to close. The eyes that stared fixedly at an object without blinking. The eyes that looked but did not see. A nose that automatically breathed because it had to. I was a totally different person, a person who never knew herself before. A person who lived without soul, without instinct, without voice or morals. A person who waited to die or to be executed at any time.

My grandmother's commune leader agreed to let Mouch and me move to my grandmother's commune while my brother Nal and the other young siblings stayed at Father's commune in Ken Dieng. Agreeing to let us move did not mean that we could stay with my grandmother, however. My sister and I had to stay with a girls team, the "student team," at a temple about three kilometers from where my grandmother lived.

The day I moved in with the student team, someone stole a pumpkin that belonged to the group. During the nightly meeting before bed, I was confronted about stealing the pumpkin. The *Mekang* gave me a first warning. There was nothing to say to the group except that I did not do it. The next day, I was questioned by the team leader, Roeun. Finally, a week later a girl in another group confessed.

Although it was close to the harvest season, the student team was starving. Some rice crops ripened early, but that was not enough to save the villagers' lives. The group members who had parents nearby sneaked home at night and came back to the temple in the morning. Sometimes the whole building was almost empty. No group leader or soldiers watched us. As Old People, most of the girls in the group had the privilege of a private kitchen and food at home. They went to stay with their families and enjoyed a good meal. Their parents saved food for them. As long as they went to see their parents, the girls were never tired of walking, even a million miles away. What about my sister and me? As New People, we starved. We got whatever Angkar ordered. We went to our grandparents' place just to see them and say hello.

A couple of weeks later, Grandmother was getting better and taking care of Grandfather. There was not enough food at the commune's main kitchen. My youngest sister cried from hunger, but she was happy to see me. She thought that I had brought food for her. As soon as Grandmother saw me, she yelled, "Go away—I have no food for you. You just come and eat my food. You never bring any food for us."

She added, "Go back, the soldiers may be looking for you!" I looked at my sister and my grandfather, who were lying on the bamboo bed. In their eyes I read many meanings. I thought I had a place to come home to, but I did not. I decided to go back to the temple with an empty stomach. I completely understood that my grandmother's unkindness was due to hunger. She had always been kind and cared about her grandchildren.

∾

A few girls at the temple, including me and my sister, had no place to go. I could not sleep because of the hunger. My nose smelled food and my eyes saw it in front of me. It was hard to lie down and hard to sit, and hard to move my body because my sharp tailbone hurt so much. I could not stand because of dizziness. My legs, hands, and face were swollen, and I could see clear water under my dark, jaundiced skin. I was half alive and half dead. I was indifferent to day or night.

Mouch was stronger than I. She found some crabs and fish and made a soup for me to eat. She encouraged me to go with her to look for vegetables so we could live for another hour. She taught me how to hunt for crabs and fish. We made a good team. I learned to find vegetables, and she was an expert at finding crabs. We cooked and ate together. At night we used our mosquito net to catch fish and shrimp. We exchanged shrimp for salt. Our rations improved. I gave some of my food to friends who lay in bed waiting for food.

One day, the *Ka-Nak-Sa-Hak-Kaor* announced that Angkar needed a volunteer team to harvest the rice crop along Tonle Sap Lake. He promised to give us rice. I was the first to volunteer. I hated living in the commune. I wanted to get as far away as I could.

The new team was called to the harvest. When we finished, Angkar threw a party for the team by giving us a big meal of rice and beef stew, and each person received twelve packs of cigarettes. I swallowed the rice. I had almost forgotten how to eat rice without broth. I had drunk soup for two years. But this was real, substantial *rice*. Then I thought about my father. I stopped swallowing the rice and just thought about him for a moment. I had plenty of rice to eat and twelve packs of cigarettes. Behind me, some girls screamed. I glanced back and saw them fall to the ground. They had eaten too much rice and their stomachs could not adjust. I told my sister to stop eating right away to prevent her stomach from being overwhelmed. This was another way of killing people, without guns or knives. It was a silent killing by rice.

In January 1977, our team reached Kanh Chor village, where my father had lived before marrying my mother. I was curious about the people in this village. I asked them about my father. Everyone knew him and told me how good, kind, and gentle he was.

We slept on the grass near the village. In the middle of the night, it poured rain. With no place to hide, we had no choice but to try to sleep in the rain. We were close to Tonle Sap Lake, and I could hear cobras slithering nearby. At 5:00 the next morning, the leader whistled and we all got up and went to the field, even though our clothes were soaking wet. Luckily, the leader called on me to cook for our team. I was glad I didn't have to work in the field, but I had a hard time finding wood for cooking because of the heavy rain.

My decision to volunteer away from my village helped me survive for another three months. This team had enough rice to eat. We also got beef, pork, fish, and dessert once a week. I gained about twenty-five pounds. I felt like a chick hatched from its egg, with my new pink face and beautiful skin. I was a human again, thanks to the power of rice. Working as a cook, I filled myself up with whatever food was available. Every girl looked like an angel out of nowhere. After working hard all day, the girls danced and sang the Communist songs. I heard a lot of laughter every night. Every one thanked Angkar for this kindness.

I looked at the stars and moon at night and wondered when a new regime would come. I was no longer afraid of the soldiers. The killing and executions had slowed down for a little while.

But some girls died from a cobra bite, which scared us. There was no medicine to cure a poisonous snake bite. Besides this, evil spirits such as Neak Ta Prey, and ghosts sometimes bothered people.

In early April 1977, my team returned to my village after Angkar declared an "excellent job done" in harvesting hundreds of acres of rice. My reward was to stay with my family for one day.

I went to see my grandparents and my youngest sister. Grandmother, surrounded by aunts and uncles and neighbors, informed me of what she called the good news: "I've engaged you to Neam while you were out with your team." She smiled. "I want to see you get married, so you can stay in the village. You won't have to travel, and you can take care of your siblings," she said.

Neam was my friend Meng's brother and a former high school teacher He was seven years older than me. When I was growing up, they lived five houses down from us.

Everyone looked at me for my answer. I did not want to say no in front of my grandmother.

"Rina is a very good granddaughter," she said. "In the absence of her parents, I am the one who makes the decision about whether she is going to be married, right?"

I had no intention of getting married in this situation. Staying in the village was not my plan, either.

"Neam works in a fishery group in Tonle Sap. He has fish to eat and he can help you and your siblings survive," my grandmother continued, enthusiastically describing my happy future with Neam. Under the Communist regime, jobs in a few areas were considered lucky: fishing, sugar processing, farming, and ricekeeping.

My grandmother was best friends with Neam's mother. They worked together making mats used for drying rice. That's where they came up with the idea to engage me to Neam. I remembered how I used to ride on Neam's shoulders while I played with Meng. Neam's family was very poor, but he made his way through school to become a high school teacher. He was a nice man who cared about his family. He was a hard worker. He would make a good husband, but I did not want to marry him under these circumstances. I had lost any feelings of love and passion for him. I foresaw only separation or death if we got married, because as "educated persons," we were targets for execution.

"What is your answer, Rina?" my aunt asked me.

"It's up to Grandmother!" I answered.

My grandmother was proud of me. "See, I tell you, Rina is a good daughter. Good daughters always follow elders' advice."

I left them to go back to the temple where my team was staying. I let them enjoy their discussion of my miserable future. My one free day was wasted. Instead of enjoying it, I had to think of ways to avoid getting married. One thing I believed in was destiny. If we were meant to be a happily married couple, we would meet again someday.

During the summer of 1977, Angkar allowed anyone in my village, old and young, to get married. Weddings took place every weekend for thirty to fifty couples. Many parents forced their daughters to get married so they could stay and work in the village commune. Some of the girls on my team said good-bye to us to start their new lives as married women.

Later, Angkar eliminated the option of letting families make decisions about marriage. The regime set up its own way for girls and boys to be married—arranging marriages without letting boys and girls know who their husband or wife would be. Twenty to fifty couples would be married in one day. After a wedding, at night soldiers would listen outside the new couple's hut to see how well they were getting along. If they got along, the couple would be fine. If not, there would be a commune meeting to criticize them. If the couple could not work it out, both people were executed.

One day I met an old man who was helping my group fix baskets. He knew a lot about Buddhist fortune-telling and other things. I asked him to tell me my future. He told me that I must be engaged, but Neam was not the man of my dreams. He assured me that Neam was not a good partner.

Neam's mother wanted us to get married soon. My sister and my teammates teased me all week long. My team leader did not know how to read or write, so she asked me to read the list of boys and girls for this week's wedding. When she handed me the list, my heart almost dropped to the ground. My name was on the list to be married to Neam. I was getting sweaty, and my hands were trembling. I decided to take a risk to save myself. I crossed out my name and wrote a new list for her to send to Angkar for approval. I did not hate Neam, but I refused to get married with the Communist regime still in power.

Neam's mother's lost the battle to get her son married. Problems arose between my grandmother and Neam's mother, especially when she learned that Angkar had completely closed the wedding season. She would have to wait another year. I declared my victory. And I volunteered to work outside the village again.

On August 28, 1977, my girls team was sent on a regional dam operation, crossing from Pursat River to Battambang Province. Angkar assigned my group to Dang Kear village, about a kilometer from my house in Pursat. My group leader appointed me and my friend Pep to cook for the group four weeks in a row. This was the best job I'd ever had. Pep and I were good cooks and worked hard to find vegetables so the group had enough food to eat. All the group members asked to have us cook again and again.

While looking for wood and vegetables one day, I met another cook from a different commune. She told me about a network to help people escape to Thailand, organized by ex-government soldiers. According to Voice of America radio reports, the first group had reached the Thai border yesterday. A second group would be leaving next week. If I wanted to go, she would meet me here at 8:00 that evening.

"Think about it," she said, then quickly disappeared.

This gave me much to consider. If I could reach the Thai

border, I could ask Mike for help. I was so nervous. I thought about Mouch, my team, and the trip. Could I trust the girl who'd given me the information? The day passed very quickly and seemed to force me to make a decision. I did not share my thoughts with anyone, not even my sister.

In my nervousness, I was unable to help with the cooking that day. I decided to meet the lady tonight at 8:00 at the same place where I'd seen her before, at my old house. I counted every minute that passed. It was 5:45 P.M. . . . 6:00 . . . . 6:15 . . . . 6:30 . . . . . I wore two pairs of pants and two shirts. In each pant pocket, I put dry rice. I wore my kramar, planning to take a bath in a nearby well. The wind blew my short hair softly and gently back and forth. My eyes were tired but I tried not to fall to sleep. The wind in my hair felt so comfortable. Then I felt my father's hand caress my forehead.

Suddenly I woke up, panicked to see many people around me. I asked them what was going on. Mouch told me that I had a temperature of 105. I asked what time it was. She said it was 8:30 P.M. I cried because I had missed the chance of my life. I imagined the trip with the girl I had met. I was very disappointed and sorry.

On Sunday, October 5, 1977, there was a general assembly for Region #7, presented by a regional leader named Soth. All the girls' and boys' teams marched in black uniform. This was the second time I had seen Mr. Soth in person. The first time I had seen him was when he gave the speech at my high school in 1975.

This was a national meeting to convey a message of kindness from Angkar to the work teams. Through Mr. Soth, Angkar declared this day a national holiday, and any mistakes that girls and boys had made would be excused. Most of the problems happened among "students" who still carried remnants of American imperialism.

I was afraid because of what I had talked about with the girl from the other commune. I was suspicious of what was going on. After Mr. Soth's speech, a short man in a soldier's uniform with a red and pink striped kramar went to the microphone and announced, "I want you boys and girls to confess and apologize to Angkar for what you did."

I had no saliva to swallow, my mouth was so dry. My eyes were wide open to see who was on the stage. Right away I saw the girl whom I had met at my house. Oh God, she must have reported me to Angkar. My life would end in the next hour. I covered my face with my kramar, except my eyes.

A man in the first row stood up and said, "My name is Sean. I was a sophomore at the Pharmacy Faculty in Phnom Penh. I would like to confess that I complained about how badly Angkar treated people. I was still influenced by American imperialism, but now I swear that Angkar is my kindest parent, who takes care of people. Please accept my apologies, Angkar. I promise that I will prepare my mind and soul to be ready for Angkar."

A woman in baggy black clothes with a kramar that showed she was New People originally from Phnom Penh, declared, "My name is Roeun, a former medical student at the University of Phnom Penh. I would like to confess that I complained how bad Angkar was to people. I was influenced by American imperialism, but now I swear that Angkar is my kindest parent, who takes care of people. Please accept my apologies, Angkar. I promise that I will prepare my mind and soul to be ready for Angkar."

The speeches went on: "My name is Phy, and I was a student at the Law Faculty in Phnom Penh. Because I carried remnants of American imperialism, my group and I made a big mistake and joined Angkar's enemy to escape to Thailand. Angkar showed goodness and saved my life from the Americans, our enemy. Now I am determined to follow Angkar to destroy the American network. Long live Angkar!" The audience applauded.

Angkar considered many boys and girls to be "mentally ill." The soldiers called these people to stand in line. One by one, the students told about their mistakes. Then it was my group's turn. There were thirteen students in my group, ranging from seventh to twelfth grade. Four of my classmates were called to line up: Suy Sovann, Cheung Kolo, Trung Pech, and Min Mealnary. I was the last one in the row. Pep sat in front of me. I held my breath and got ready to stand up. But the soldier skipped to another group. I was released.

CHAPTER 12

Hell

TWO WEEKS AFTER THE OFFICIAL MEETING, I was struck with severe stomach pain. I was sent to the regional hospital in Pursat City. The hospital was set up in the elementary school where my father used to teach. It was difficult to get into the hospital without the help of the Old People. My group leader, one of the Old People, found an oxcart to carry me to the hospital. As my pain escalated, I grabbed her hand for help. The group leader dropped me at the hospital. She covered my shoulders with her silk kramar to keep me from getting chilled.

∽

At the hospital, when the nurse in charge saw that I had a silk kramar, she put me in the Old People's building. Old People were treated differently than New People. They received more medicine, food, and care. In the Old People's building, I heard soldiers' wives talking about how to fight Lon Nol's soldiers, how to execute New People, how to spot educated persons, and how to get Old People privileges. Many of these stories had been passed from one patient to another. The doctor told me that my appendix was touching the left side of my stomach. I would have to have surgery to remove the appendix. But I had heard the soldiers' wives talking about how the doctors used a small regular knife during surgery, so I didn't want to do it. I asked to return to my work team, but my group had already been sent back to the village. The nurse in charge would not let me go.

❧

The next week, a doctor was scheduled to operate on two female soldiers with appendicitis. After their operations, the women had some intestinal problems. The doctor canceled my operation so he could study my symptoms more. I was lucky. I asked to go out to the village again. This time I gave the right reason, referring to Angkar's goodness. The nurse believed me and let me go home. She even gave me some rice to eat on the way. Wow! The privilege of being Old People—no wonder they did not give up power easily.

As soon as I reached my grandmother's hut, she informed me of my disengagement. "Neam's mother told me that she does not want Neam to marry you anymore. She wanted someone who could marry her son sooner," she said sadly, in a low voice. "She said that if someone else wants to be engaged to you, you are free to do that," she added.

"That's all right, Grandma. She has no right to tell me who I should marry. It's good that we aren't engaged. Marrying him was not my idea. If I get married I'll have to raise my family, and who would help you?" I said. "Actually, I didn't want to hurt your feelings by saying no, Grandma. I just did it to please you."

I felt so happy to be a free girl again. But for Grandma, it brought shame and disgrace to the family because girls usually disengaged from boys. When a man became unengaged first, it meant there was something wrong with the woman.

I stayed with Grandma for a couple of days. At lunch in the main kitchen one day, the commune leader, Roeun, came with Ta Oum, who used to live next door to me, and announced that he needed five or six girls to work at the fishery at Tonle Sap. I volunteered and asked Mouch to come with me on this new assignment. She asked me how I was going to face Neam at Tonle

Sap. I told her that I would have nothing to do with him. His mother had clearly informed me of the broken engagement. I was going there to work—maybe I would get some fish to send home—and to stay away from the village as much as possible. I had heard about Tonle Sap but had never been there. I thought of this as my big adventure, and I just wanted to be free from this regime. Maybe I could find a way to the Thai border by crossing Siem Reap Province.

On November 30, 1977, my sister and I and four other girls went to Tonle Sap. Two oxcarts carried our group and supplies. It took us all day to reach the lake. The trip was haunted by a mountain of soldiers' bones and skulls that we passed. The men had been executed in Pra Chrey in early 1975. A strong stench still emanated from the heap. Skulls, leg and arm bones, knees, and fingers were scattered everywhere.

A big sailboat was waiting near the shore of the lake. It seemed that people had prepared a celebration for our arrival. A men's group was waiting for us, smiling and welcoming us from the ox-cart. Neam was among them. I heard a lot of teasing and laughing. I hadn't had feelings like these for a long, long time.

I saw Neam every day at work, lunch, and meetings but never talked to or looked at him, which made the group stop teasing us and wonder what was going on. Neam had always cared about me and my sister.

A week later, he asked my sister, "Mouch, doesn't Rina talk to me or even look at me? What's wrong?"

"How dare you ask that question?" she said. "I think you are a respectable gentleman—why did you do this to my sister?"

"Do what to your sister?" he replied quickly.

"You were engaged to my sister, then you broke the engagement off! The worst thing is, you sent a message that Rina was free to marry someone else. How can you look me in the face?" my sister yelled.

"My mother! Disengage me without telling me?" Neam was

very upset. "Sorry, I didn't know anything about it. Let Rina know that I had nothing to do with that!"

My sister ran to find me in the boat and told me what Neam said. I was not interested.

The next day, I heard that Neam asked permission from his leader to go to the village to make a new pact with Grandma. The group leader gave him some fish to bring to Grandma as an apology. Three days later, my sister brought green and ripe mangoes for me. I refused to touch them, but Mouch ate them all. That night, Ta Oum brought a message from Neam that he did apologize to Grandma and asked her to forgive him and his mother. He told Grandma that he loved me and did not mean to hurt my family at all. Grandma accepted apologies easily, I knew that. She encouraged him to ask me if he could apologize to me for his mistake. Through our mediator Ta Oum, I said nothing, which he interpreted to mean that it was OK.

Neam was a happy man again. His group started teasing him again and made jokes about him. They called him Anh Tih San and me Neang Mom, characters in a soap opera called "A Country Girl." Neam always sent me extra food he found at work. I never took a bite, but my sister ate all of it.

I spent most of my free time after work in the peninsula in the lake, enjoying nature. Oh, Tonle Sap, I had heard your name in my geography class, but never met you in person. You are rich in fish, surrounded by dark green bushes, your beautiful water reaches the skyline. Many wild birds competed to dive for the fish that were stuck in the mud after the tide went out. Not far from my side, an otter swam up and down to catch fish, so abundant in this lake. The rays of the sunset reflected off the water. The fresh breeze blowing across the water touched the bushes and made a soft music. I felt safe, which I hadn't felt for so long. I realized that I had suffered for a long time and had even had a mental breakdown. Now, with nature surrounding me, I felt alive again, like an unhealthy plant just watered by a fresh dew or rain. But I did not know how long this moment would last.

❧

I learned all the ways fishermen looked for, trapped, and caught fish, turtles, and eels. Two things I remember very well are finding a python in my boat and being in a storm on the middle of Tonle Sap. Ta Oum told me that if I saw anything strange, I should keep my mouth shut because I might curse the spirit in charge of Tonle Sap. I did see the storm twist the water out of the lake into a funnel.

At the end of May 1978, our group returned to the village. I learned the sad news that my third brother, No, was in jail. He was just twelve years old. No was arrested for criticizing the Communist regime and put in jail near the orphanage. No was the youngest prisoner. The first night he was arrested, soldiers brought him into a dark house full of adult prisoners. Most of them were middle-aged men. No described the jail as a big, old haunted house: very dark, no open windows. The entire house was filled with urine and feces. The soldier pulled his arm and No tripped over an inmate's leg. When he was left with the other inmates, a voice whispered in his ear and asked him who he was. He mentioned my father's name, and the men felt pity for him. They admired the many good things my father done for the villagers.

No worked so hard to adjust to being an inmate. But no matter how hard he worked, how good his behavior was, the soldiers always found fault with him. In the late afternoon one day, another inmate sneaked away while doing a chore for the Khmer Rouge soldiers and came to my grandmother's hut. He told her, "No was shot and killed last week." My grandmother screamed, "He was an innocent kid!" I lay on the hammock, my clothes dirty from working in the rice field. "How did they kill him?" I cried.

"The soldier, who was about No's age, was cleaning his gun.

He asked No if his gun was loaded or unloaded. No answered, 'I don't know, my friend.' 'If you don't know, raise your arms,' the soldier commanded. No rose his arms up and smiled while the soldier shot him three times. He fell to the ground bleeding."

My brother's sudden death in jail happened on September 8, 1978, when he was twelve years old. I had no way to find his body.

In late 1978, there was another large evacuation of people from the east to our area. These people were easy to get along with and easy to recognize by their blue and green kramars, the colors designated by Angkar for people from the east. They were also recognizable by their accent. Out of curiosity, I asked them, "Why did Angkar send you over here? How was life in your village?" They said that Vietnamese forces had invaded Svay Rieng Province, and Western soldiers were attacking them as the Communist enemy. The refugees gave me an overview of the situation, the conclusion of which was the continuation of the Communists' mass killings.

Not long after my brother's death, Angkar ordered my work team to dig a dam in Sam San, a mountainous region about 100 kilometers from where we lived. Sam San was totally jungle. Many giant trees were nearly a hundred years old. There were a couple of small villages in the area with about twenty to thirty families. The area was very dry. Two or three ponds supplied a limited amount of water. No vegetables grew for us to live on. Sam San was a dead-end place, and I felt that my life would end here.

Each day the sound of bombs and guns seemed to be coming closer and closer, giving us a sense of hope that we might be rescued from the tiger's mouth. Khmer Rouge soldiers, male and female, came and went in their uniforms. Others stored tanks, trucks, weapons, and food near my workplace. More healthy families and children in black clothes and black Ho Chi Minh sandals continued to arrive in oxcarts and truck convoys. I observed their movements and sometimes had a chance to listen to their conversations. These new arrivals were soldiers' families that came from northern Cambodia.

The Khmer Rouge radio still played the same music and continued to declare their victory over American imperialism. The discrepancy between the radio announcements and the soldiers moving in and out made me wonder what would happen. Rumors about a new government spread very fast in the work team. Everyone knew something but could not learn the truth.

A quiet young man named Phin held the position of ordering food, wood, and bamboo for Angkar. Though he was New People, Phin was very popular among Old People, and very healthy compared to the other boys, girls, and adults. Old People liked to tease him just to see him smile, with his double dimples to the left of a dark mole with a single long black hair, which he often tugged to get attention. Phin was the only man with the authority to travel and communicate with other communities and regions.

Phin lived a couple of huts away from the girls team, so I saw him often. I noticed that lately he seemed more relaxed and smiled more than in the past. Sometimes he glanced at me with a different look, but it was not love or friendship. He seemed to want to tell me something. Sometimes I wondered, who was this man?

Work was going as usual. My sister and I had the assignment of each digging five cubes of dirt a day. If we completed our job before sunset, we got extra rice at supper. Two baskets, long bamboo sticks, and a long hoe were my best friends. I carried fifty kilograms of dirt on each shoulder, with one basket on the left and one on the right. I walked about a hundred yards to dump the dirt onto a new road that was being built. My right shoulder became swollen and numb. I took turns with my sister carrying dirt. She dug the dirt with a hoe. I carried dirt. When she carried, I dug. My two palms were numb and the skin was very rough.

When I put my hands on my face to clean in the morning, I could feel the rough cuts in the skin.

In January 1979, on the way out for lunch on a very hot day, the boys and girls teams walked side by side with a soldier who was carrying a radio. The station was playing a patriotic song of Angkar. The soldier handed the radio to me to hold while he looked for his cigarette, which he'd dropped on the ground. The radio frequency seemed scrambled for a moment, then I heard, "We took over at Stung Mein Chey radio station. . . ." The voice disappeared by the time the soldier pulled the radio from my hand. But the crowd of boys and girls had heard it. We looked at each other, almost cheered out loud, but tried to remain calm.

I was anxious to know who this "we" was on the radio—the Cambodian ex-government? American-backed Cambodians? Who were they? Every day I went to work and waited to be rescued. My sister, on the other hand, had a connection with some Old People whom she considered a godmother and godsister. They liked Mouch and gave her extra food and sugar palm and bribed the *Mekang* to count her as a regular worker. She was not aware of what went on outside the team—she cared only about food.

One day passed and then another, and nothing happened after the broadcast on the radio. Commune leaders held a meeting to inform us that Angkar needed more wells dug immediately. The boys and girls teams competed with each other for a reward of rice. For two days and two nights we worked nonstop, digging many deep wells.

A lot of things happened coincidentally. In another commune, Angkar forced many boys and girls to marry. Everyone was forced to work longer hours, and soldiers killed those who refused to follow orders. The first priority for execution were people from the east, then educated people, and finally people who disobeyed Angkar's rules. A few men, women, and children escaped from the team every day. In every meeting, the soldiers announced their capture and executed them.

At the end of January was the darkest night of the month; not a single star appeared in the sky. Food was served early, before six o'clock. Each team meeting finished early. Late that evening, we heard running and footsteps. The footsteps disappeared but horrible voices cried for help. We heard the sharp tone of a girl calling from the distance, "Injustice! Killing human life." Her screams faded with the sound of beating.

Her cry was intolerable. Every girl in my group urinated unconsciously. The stench of fresh blood entered the room with a soldier who flashed a light on all the girls, who pretended to be asleep. We mentally followed his footsteps toward his girlfriend. He pulled her out of sleep to clean his stinking body, bloody from killing innocent people. The flashlight illuminated his half-bald forehead, which indicated that he was a former Buddhist monk. He was full of blood from head to his toes. Laughing, he described how difficult it was to slit the throat of a woman who would not separate from her newlywed husband. The soldiers involved in these executions pulled the clothes from girls and boys before killing them. In their generosity, the soldiers gave the clothes to my team as a gift.

I could not sleep the whole night as I tried to find a way to escape this hell. I was sure I would be next on the list. Angkar kept only people who sacrificed everything, body and soul, for Angkar. I did not think Angkar counted me as one of his.

In the morning, my *Mekang* ordered me to work at a different site. I heard that a well at my work site was filled with dead bodies. The two huts of the new arrivals from Svay Rieng were very quiet. A trail of blood stained the leaves everywhere. A long wooden bat and stick still had a bloody fingerprint. This gave me a clear picture of last night's scenario.

Phin, the supply man, approached me and quietly mentioned

that Pursat City was occupied by a new government that had claimed victory in Phnom Penh recently. The Khmer Rouge had prohibited his supply group from going in the direction of Pursat City. Phin said the group that escaped to Pursat last week was safe. But Angkar had announced their execution to scare people and keep us from running.

"Meet me at the eastside pond tomorrow before sunset. Say nothing, bring nothing," he said when we passed each other at lunch.

Starvation was not my problem anymore. I had lost my appetite. I was short of breath, my heart pounding. I imagined all the different risks that running entailed. In spite of the risks, I had to take the chance. I thought, "If it is not my time, I will not die," to calm myself. I wasn't sure whether to bring Mouch with me. If something happened to her, it would be my fault. I talked with her, and she volunteered to go.

When the time came, Phin carried his sharp, long-handled knife used for cutting plants. He walked past my team's hut toward the eastside pond. I gave a signal to my sister and pretended to go take a bath at the pond. Before leaving, I prayed for my parents' souls to protect me.

At the meeting place I found Phin, along with other men from the adult group and one of the men's sisters. Phin had planned this escape for a long time while working as commuter for the commune. He would be our guide. Everyone trusted him because he knew the trails, routes, and villages on the way to Pursat. We would reach the city in a week, if we encountered no obstacles along the way.

CHAPTER 13

A Way Out

ON FEBRUARY 8, 1979, JUST BEFORE SUNSET, my escape group started out toward Pursat. There were twelve of us in the group. We would travel by night and hide during the day. Phin gave us the rules: Be extra aware when crossing streets, villages, and farms. Spread apart from each other and hide if you see or hear anything suspicious. A double whistle from Phin means to look for a hiding place. When approaching a village, tiptoe if possible. Never leave a member behind, no matter what. There were two dangerous places that might be guarded by soldiers. One was Talo village, a Khmer Rouge base, and the other was a railroad near National Route 5.

Darkness fell and dew started to form into fog. After we had walked for about two hours, we began to wonder if the soldiers had realized yet that our group had run away from the team. We were worried that they would send an alert to the troops in Talo or another village ahead of us. Suddenly, Phin whispered to get down on the ground in the rice field. Five soldiers holding guns on their shoulders walked along the dike in front of us. Terrified, I wondered why the soldiers did not see us and how Phin could have seen them in the dark. I hadn't seen them.

Our goal for tonight was to get through Talo as fast as possible. We walked toward the village. On an unpaved road ahead of us, we saw the headlights of a couple of trucks coming toward us. Phin told us to run across the road after the last truck passed.

As soon as the last truck drove by, we all rushed into the dusk, as thick as chimney smoke.

As we were running, I stepped into a deep, open hole filled with corpses—the grave of some recently executed people. My feet sank deeper and deeper, up to my knees. I could feel small creatures crawling on my skin. Some kind of oil or liquid moved under my bare feet, and I felt a human bone touching my toes. An awful stench rose around me. I could barely pull myself out of the grave. I was the last one to reach the group. We stopped for drinking water, and I cleaned my feet. Phin told us how to find our way to Pursat in case we got lost. I held my sister's hand very tight, afraid of losing her.

"The crocodile stars will bring us to Pursat," Phin said. He pointed to a constellation in the shape of a crocodile.

"We're coming up to major road that we need to cross. Get ready to run," he said. We followed his order by running together across the road. In the middle of the road, Phin spotted some soldiers. Spreading apart was one of our rules. My sister loosened her hand from mine. I lowered myself silently into the water alongside the road. I heard footsteps above my head, then a dropping noise in front of me. I closed both eyes and prayed. My body was shaking. A long, slippery leech circled my ankle and sucked my blood. Two soldiers shined a flashlight ahead of them. As soon as they walked past me, I rushed to pull the leech from my ankle. Then I looked for my sister. I couldn't find her. I ran around in the dark looking for her.

"Mouch! Mouch! Where are you?" I called.

I found her with Phin and the others. Trees full of thorns had ripped my shirt, pants, and kramar into pieces. My face was scratched and my feet were bleeding from stepping on thorns. My body felt cramped.

Around midnight, the moon showed up clearly, so it was easy to walk through the jungle. We thought we were in a temporary safe zone. We found many bundles of rice on plants waiting to be harvested. We spread our kramars on the ground and shook the rice bundles over them. Rice grains dropped from the stems. Each of us carried some rice for the next day.

After walking all night, past Talo village, we reached a couple of haystacks in the middle of a large rice field. We made holes in the mountains of hay and climbed into them. My body started to cramp and ache badly. My feet were full of broken thorns from running on bare feet. My sister used a thorn to pulled the broken pieces from my skin. We woke up around three o'clock in the afternoon, ate our leftover food, and prepared for the next stage of our trip. After surviving last night, I had overcome my fear.

When night came, we continued to follow the crocodile stars. We did not see any soldiers. But we were prepared and were aware of any villagers who passed us. We came to a field filled with watermelons. We sat in a circle, eating as much as we could because this was the first time that we had eaten freely. Then we cooked rice for that night and the next day. Someone made a fire. Someone else brought water. Some cooked. Some smashed rice grains for a rainy day. Eating all the rice we could was a freedom we deserved. No one controlled us. We continued with our plan. We fled at night and rested during the day.

❧

On the third and fourth nights, we got lost by a river, which we assumed was Svay Doun Keo, thirty kilometers from Pursat. There was no way to avoid the river. On the other side, an oxcart team carried rice in the opposite direction. We tried and tried but could not find a way to cross the deep river. While everyone rested, Phin climbed to the top of a tree to look for a shallow zone in the river where we could cross. Fortunately, he found one.

❧

The fifth night, our goal was to cross the river. Phin walked toward the place he thought might be shallow. My sister and I did not worry about drowning because we knew how to swim. During February, it was still quite chilly at night, so the water was freezing. Phin was right—the water was only about five feet deep in this spot. Our members moved quietly across the calm water under a full moon.

Soon after I reached the opposite bank, the sound of gunfire rang toward us. Everyone spread out, rushed out of the water, and hid in bushes. We were not surprised by this shooting but were prepared every moment for a situation like this.

We crossed rice fields, farms, and jungles in the middle of the night. Hearing a wolf howling in the distance alerted us to the possibility of a mass grave nearby. The dew was getting heavier and heavier and made us very cold. Some people in the group had the flu and fever. Because we had to avoid villages, rivers, and other places, it was taking us longer than we expected to reach the city.

On the seventh night, Phin put his ear to the ground and asked us to take a break because he heard something unusual—many heavy steps.

"A herd of elephants is ahead of us—wait until they pass," he said.

While we took a break, some men climbed up in a tree to guard us. Others cooked rice. Some girls lay down to rest. Phin joined me and told me the story of how he had escaped from one place to another.

"After my parents died, I went to join a boys team," he began. "At the orphanage where I lived, I fell in love with a girl from Phnom Penh. When she was three months pregnant, we asked Angkar for permission to get married, but after finding out that she was pregnant, the soldiers set up a meeting for her execution." He paused, taking a deep breath, and looked to the ground. "Soldiers beat her up, stabbed her, cut her wrist and throat, and buried her alive." He pulled his cigarette out of his mouth while blowing smoke into the sky. "After the soldiers left the scene, I rushed to dig her out of the ground. She was dead, completely dead," he continued, "but her body was still warm, warm like . . . when she was with me, that kind of warm. . . ." He put his cigarette back in his mouth. "I lay her body in the ground, pulled out my pocket knife, cut through her tummy, and pulled the fetus out of it . . ." I was suddenly wide awake, stunned by what he was telling me. "I rolled the fetus in my magical cloth, which protects me from danger, went home, and grilled . . ." he stopped speaking when someone brought us some cooked rice to eat.

I feared that it was a mistake to escape with this man. Who was he exactly? I was scared of him and wondered what other things he could do.

On the ninth night, we continued to follow the crocodile stars, avoiding a village. The sun sneaked his head up, sending a jaundiced ray to tell us that morning would soon come. We were in the middle of a rice field, with hardly any bushes to hide in. About a kilometer ahead of us was one medium-size tree and a small bush. We decided to use them as a hiding place. The tree could hold up to five people and the rest of the group could stay in the bush.

That day, the sun was extremely hot—we could see the humidity thick in the air. We were very thirsty. My sister cried that she would die from the heat. She could not sleep, and kept crying so she could drink her tears to quench her thirst. I felt just as bad but did not want to show my weakness. It was a long, long day. Finally, to save our lives, Phin asked everyone who was willing to drink urine.

As soon as the sun set, everyone rushed to find water to drink. I found some dark yellow water in a small hole and eagerly sucked it into my mouth. I swallowed a mouthful of buffalo urine and poop.

We were close to Pursat. But in our exhaustion, we fell asleep in a potato field.

"Get up! Why are you sleeping in the bushes like this? Get

lost—go someplace else. Go!" An old man standing with his knife woke us up.

We came out of a deep sleep to find ourselves in the middle of a farm. We hurried to find someplace to hide. Phin observed that the only way to get off the farm was to walk through two shelter halls. About ten to fifteen people guarded this farm.

We waited until the farmer went to sleep. It was almost midnight, and the people in the shelter were still up, talking and joking. A puppy kept barking and barking. Our strategy was to walk across the shelter to the rice field so we could make a shortcut to the city.

❧

After midnight, in spite of the puppy barking and a couple of the farmers still talking, we took the risk of tiptoeing past the shelters. The puppy barked and barked until a groaning voice from the shelter calmed it down. Most of the farmers were asleep.

After crossing the farm successfully, we walked toward the rice field. Ahead, we could see a long dark railroad line. Phin discussed how we were going to cross the railroad and National Route 5, the most dangerous part of our route. He suggested that we walk in a line in case of security guards or mine explosions. In case of emergency, the people at the back of the line would immediately hide.

Phin went ahead by himself to observe the situation. It was an hour before he sent an OK signal. We walked in line as planned and peacefully crossed the railroad tracks. Then we waited another half hour to cross National Route 5. Both the railroad and the highway seemed very quiet. No one guarded them. Passing these two zones safely gave us hope that we would be heading home the next night.

We crossed another village, which was empty. It seemed like the villagers had recently fled, leaving behind all their farm animals, such as pigs, roosters, chickens, and ducks. Some men in our group caught chickens and twisted their necks. Some picked sugar cane and other food. Some found fine rice, regular and sweet. A stack of rice bags and a big jar of sugar palm were in the shelter hall, as if ready to send out somewhere. We grabbed all the rice we could carry. Leaving the village, we looked for a better place to hide. I still wondered who had taken power. Where had all the people gone? We decided to rest near a small pond about a kilometer outside the village.

That night we enjoyed rice, chicken soup, and a dessert of sweet rice and sugar palm. We had not had this much food to eat since before the Khmer Rouge took power.

The next day, while my friends ate food left over from the night before, I climbed a tree. I saw that this was the place where Angkar had held the big meeting for students to apologize. Why did the villagers leave? Where had they gone? Was my grandma's village like this? I was asking myself all these questions when a girl screamed from the bushes below me. I saw a man beat the girl and slap her face, then they hit each other. Finally, the man pulled out his pocketknife and tried to slash the girl's face.

"You cannot do whatever you want," he said to the girl. "I'm the one who tells you what to do and how to do it." She tried to escape but he pulled her shirt off and hit her until she was unconscious. Then he lowered her to the ground, pulled his pants off, and raped her. I was trembling and sweating. I almost fell from the tree. Oh god! It was Phin—raping Ouk, the oldest girl in our escape team.

After the rape, Ouk was still unconscious. Phin pulled himself out of her, covered her body with a kramar, and sat at the edge of her feet smoking a cigarette. I was stunned. My body was paralyzed, my breath short, and my eyes closed. If Phin glanced up, he would see me and kill me.

Ouk woke up and found herself naked. Blood from her scratches dropped onto the ground by Phin, who was still sitting next to her. She cried out.

"If you tell anyone about this, I will kill you," he told Ouk with his grinning teeth. Then he left.

I wanted to ask Ouk if I could help her, but I was scared it might make things worse. Ouk calmed down, put on her ripped shirt and skirt, and walked back to the group.

Pretending to look for wood, still in a state of shock, I was out of breath and shaking. I kept this secret in my heart. I tried to erase it from my face. I was scared of Phin. I tried to encourage a couple of strong men in the group to leave but they refused to go without Phin's orders. I was very nervous but pretended I didn't know anything.

Three nights passed. Everyone seemed to enjoy the freedom of having plenty of food, the freedom of not having to work, and the freedom to sleep. Having food to eat made us forget not only the goal of reaching our families but also the risk of a mass killing. Believing in Phin, even worshipping him, the group members came up with the idea of living together as we were right now. Planning who would cook, who would find fish and vegetables, and who would be the rice keeper for our team, the group members trusted Phin one hundred percent. They believed that he had a special power that allowed him to see things we could not see. They were confident that Phin would protect us. Even Ouk herself seemed to accept this.

Phin recognized that I seemed worried about this plan. While everyone else was bathing in a small pond and looking for snails, I walked in a different direction from Phin. I wanted to avoid him. Phin started joking and teasing me about my fiancé. He told a story about an old man with a young wife, saying that the old man treated his wife as a sex slave. Everyone laughed.

Referring to my fiancé, Phin said, "His education is superb. I don't think I can compare with him, a professor, a high school professor." He talked slowly, giving me a weird look.

While he talked, I looked at Ouk to see her reaction. She glanced at her shirt and pants. Her mind was someplace else.

Phin pointed a finger toward me. "She never talked to me or looked at me when she was in high school. Ha! and now she has a fiancé who is a high school professor," he said to the group.

"Shut up! Stop teasing me!" I yelled and moved out of the circle.

"You're hurt, right? Ha! You can't stand to listen anymore," he burst out, which changed the atmosphere suddenly. It seemed like something had bothered him for a long time and this was his chance to express his anger and frustration. Who was he? Why did he know so much about me?

Everyone looked at me, expecting me to apologize. No way. He pulled out his pocketknife and stabbed a pumpkin into pieces, the way he had ripped Ouk's shirt off her.

"I think it is time for me to go back to my family," he stated to the group, looking at me angrily. "I've helped you all I can."

Hearing this, everyone panicked. Some went to appease him and some pressured me to beg him not to leave the group. He kept repeating that he was useless for the group.

Group members told him that he had a very important role and asked him not to leave the group. I was worried when night came. I thought Phin was a mysterious man—one side was a god and the other side was evil. His violence might put everyone in danger. I asked my sister to stay close and told her about my plan to leave the group. I knew exactly where I was and could find my way out without Phin's help.

That night, the group decided to continue on to the city. From here it would take us only one night to reach Pursat. After walking for three hours, Phin stopped at his house, which was destroyed, with only small pieces of wood left behind. From a distance, we could see that the electricity was on in Pursat. It was around four o'clock in the morning. Clouds were scattered across the sky, bringing a few sprinkles.

While crossing a dam, we found a water supply. A strong wind twisted my hair and blew dust into my nose and eyes. I heard a noise like footsteps running, mingled with a strong wind from the west. It was totally dark. Suddenly, the sound of gunfire came from where I'd heard the noise. Everyone ran toward the dam. From the screaming in the distance, it sounded like people were injured. I had no idea who was fighting.

I saw an opportunity for me and my sister to escape. I grabbed Mouch's hand and pushed her ahead of me to hide in a big dead tree while bullets flew overhead. Gunfire repeatedly rang out from the bushes. People ran from the direction of the bullets. A strong hand grabbed my shirt from behind, and another hand pushed me against the damp wall.

"I want you, you only, to escape with me now!" Phin whispered into my right ear.

"I can't leave my sister behind, you know that," I said.

"You have no choice—either you go with me or your sister is dead," he ordered.

While pushing me against the wall, Phin leaned his nose on my cheek and kissed me. I raised my leg enough to stand in a good position and kicked him in the crotch. He rolled away in pain. Enraged, he positioned himself to attack me with his pocketknife. I quickly grabbed his long-handled knife, which was lying next to him, and pressed it to his throat, but this was not enough to hold him still. He regained his position and slashed his pocketknife back and forth toward me. I continued to wave the long-handled knife at him. He lunged at me with his pocketknife again. I did not move fast enough, and he slashed me with the knife in a couple of places. In return, I pushed the long knife into his calf, cutting him enough so he could not make another stab at me. I had the opportunity to cut his head off, but I couldn't, I couldn't. . . . I didn't have the courage to kill him. Instead, I dropped his knife and ran to join my sister.

CHAPTER 14

Decisions

As THE GUNS CONTINUED TO FIRE between soldiers, Phin and I declared an unexpected war of hatred and revenge. My clothes were ragged, soaked with water, and bloodstained. My body hurt, and warm blood flowed from the cuts on my chest, shoulders, and arms from Phin's pocketknife.

The gunfire quieted at dawn, leaving behind a crowd of wounded civilians and people using flashlights to look for survivors. We were not far from my house in the city. From a distance, I heard people speaking in Vietnamese. I wondered what the Vietnamese were doing here.

"Who are you?" three people asked my sister and me.

"Who are you?" I asked them.

"We are Vietnamese soldiers," he answered, speaking Khmer with a Vietnamese accent.

As soon as I heard the word *Vietnamese,* I felt hopeless.

"Uncle! Do you recognize me?" my sister said to one of the men, who had been our neighbor in Pursat. "I'm Siv's daughter."

"Oh, yes, very well, my dear. What are you doing here?" the man answered.

"My sister and I escaped from Sam San but got caught in the fighting on the way to Grandma's house."

"No! No! Don't go to the village. The Khmer Rouge are evacuating people from the village—stay in the city. Your uncle Toc lives very close to my house." He discouraged us from looking for our grandmother.

The man pointed to Phin. "Who is he? Is he a Khmer Rouge trying to hurt you?" My sister looked at me and let me answer the question. Glancing at his pale sad face and sympathetic eyes, I bit my lip. My "id" urged me to say yes! yes, he is a bad person, but my "superego" gently said that revenge was not the solution.

"No, uncle, he is not a Khmer Rouge." I blew out my breath.

My sister left with a man who knew our family to find our uncle Toc.

The dawn was overtaken by the first peek of sunrise. Walking into the battlefield to observe something of last night's fighting, I found the bodies of men, women, and children dead on the ground. A couple of yards in front of me, a voice groaned, "Help! Help!" I ran toward the voice and found a person whom I could not have said was male or female because of the blood covering the body. The person held a baby with one hand and raised the other hand slowly toward me. As I approached, a clear voice called my name: "Rina! Rina! It's me, Ko . . . sal . . ."

"Kosal! Oh god. Are you all right?" I asked.

"Yes, I'm fine." He grabbed my cold hand. "I'm sorry for what I did to you. That is my sin, a sin from my previous life, a sin that separates me from you . . . maybe I deserve this . . ."

"Stop, Kosal, it's not the right time to talk about this. You'll be fine. I will look for help, Kosal."

"You're just wasting your time, Rina. Please, take care of my baby as your own, as you love me . . ." He handed me the baby, whom I hadn't seen move yet.

Blood flowed out of Kosal's chest, soaking his black shirt and his kramar. His face was pale as a white cloth. After my experiences with my mother, father, and the baby, I recognized that Kosal had been losing blood for at least two hours and his chance of survival was minute. He held my hand tighter and tighter. His eyes looked straight into mine, imploring me to live, to live for his baby, to live to tell the next generation about the genocide under the Communist regime, as he breathed his last words: "I always loved you, Rina." His hand slowly released its tight grip. His body flattened on the ground. He left me with his baby.

"No! No! Kosal, please don't leave me." I cried and screamed while hugging his baby into my chest.

A skinny old man with a dark beard and mustache stood behind me. "That is life—life is suffering. If you're alive, you have sorrow. You cannot escape that," he said. He began to remove Kosal for burial.

I wanted to talk to Kosal for just another hour. I wanted to ask him what his life was like and share with him about my life.

I stood up and walked away with his baby in my arms and cursed the world that was full of sin and suffering.

"Daughter," the old man called. "I think the baby is dead." He grabbed the baby out of my arms.

"Even an innocent baby you will not let live, God!" I cursed again, then walked away, going nowhere, trying to understand.

∾

On February 27, 1979, nineteen days after my long trip, I was reunited with my brother Ra and my uncle Toc. Toc had also escaped recently, leaving his wife and children in the Khmer Rouge zone, a remote area where the Communists had fled after the Vietnamese invasion of Cambodia on January 7, 1979. Toc had remarried, the sister of one of my girlfriends. With a friend of Uncle Toc, we all shared a big old house near Pursat City. We lived freely and celebrated our new freedom by cooking, eating, fishing, wearing bright-colored clothes. . . . Meanwhile, my grandparents and younger siblings were somewhere in the jungle in the Khmer Rouge territory.

I tried to sort out what had happened. I felt depressed thinking about my future. Financial problems were the first thing on my mind. I had no gold left and wondered how I was going to survive and raise my siblings. I ate everything I could out of nervousness, which made me gain ten pounds. Finally I looked good again.

With all these stressful thoughts floating in my head, my eyes got very heavy as I lay on the wooden floor near the wall. It was a very sunny, very steamy day. Sweat streamed off me like pouring water. I drifted off. When I woke up, I found Phin sitting on the floor by my feet, looking at me. I opened my eyes wide and sat up.

"What you doing here?"

"Why are you so mean to me?" he said. "Don't you think about our wonderful trip together? I miss that." He added, smiling at me, "Look at you, you look beautiful!"

"Don't even think of that," I cut him off. "It's not appropriate. Please leave me alone." We heard my uncle's voice from a distance.

After Phin left, my uncle questioned me about him. I felt like a little girl when my father grounded me. But I was almost twenty-two years old.

"How dare you let a man sit by your feet—what were you up to?" he scolded me in front of his wife, who was younger than I was.

"I am old enough to know what is right or wrong, Uncle. I'm not a kid anymore," I snapped back. He reacted as if I had poured gasoline on his face. "Don't you dare talk back to me like that!" He almost slapped my face in his anger. I just looked at him and his young wife and left.

It was the first bad week for me since I'd been reunited with my uncle. Problems struck from all angles—financial problems, my uncertain future, the rigid traditional culture, and the problem of how to enjoy my freedom.

At the end of the week, an unexpected guest came to see me. "Someone is waiting for you on the balcony," a neighbor told me. A man dressed in black and gray waited with his face toward the street.

I ran toward him out of curiosity. The man smiled as soon as he saw me.

"Uncle! Neam!" I exclaimed. (I used to call him the respectful term "uncle" when I was a young girl, since he was older.) "How long have you been waiting for me?" I asked.

"Not very long. So, how are you?" he replied, looking me over. "You look gorgeous!" I used to feel shy when hearing a compliment like this, but not anymore. I was mature enough to know that any flattering words from men were just words.

"I've come to ask you to marry me," Neam said. "We can find elders to help us . . . and . . ."

"I don't think it's time yet. You know I don't have my parents, and my grandparents are still with the Khmer Rouge, and it is not a good idea to marry without them," I cut him off. Upset, he said good-bye and quietly left.

That night a million things were added to my stressful list from the previous day. If I got married, I would be safe from Phin. But if I did that, I would have children, of course, and live in poverty, with no job, no money, and more and more children. Getting married was not the solution. I wanted to look for Mike, my American friend. How could I find him without his address, date of birth, and phone number?

A group of men who lived on the second floor of our house were trying to find a way to the Thai border. They had a daily meeting to consult maps and plan an escape to Thailand. I made friends with them and offered my ideas. They liked me a lot, which made my uncle and the neighbors suspect that I was having an affair with one of the men. My uncle accused me of betraying my fiancé, which just escalated the conflict between me and my uncle. He asked my brother and sister to watch me closely, and he and his wife told untrue stories about me sleeping with old men and getting pregnant out of wedlock.

With the support of Vietnamese soldiers, the Khmer soldiers

liberated people who were trapped in the Khmer Rouge zone, including my grandparents and my younger siblings. They joined us in March. I was very happy, because I wanted to talk to my grandparents before making my final decision about leaving Cambodia. The night we were reunited, I told them about Neam's marriage proposal.

"Yes, my dear, it is time for you to get married and take care of your siblings," Grandma said. "I am old now. I want to see you get married, bowing on a traditional mat in front of me, while I am still alive."

"No, I disagree." Grandpa jumped into the conversation with a definite no. I wondered what was going on between Grandpa and Neam's family. This was the second conflict between my grandparents and his family.

"Let her get married so she can take care of her siblings—do you understand that?" my grandmother said sharply to Grandpa.

Grandpa told me a story that shut Grandma up: "We were evacuated from the village with nothing. Your grandmother had a broken leg, your younger sister could not walk, your sixth and seventh siblings carried heavy loads of rice and other stuff. I had a high fever while I was taking care of everything. After hearing that you had run away with a man, Neam was enraged. He never helped your crippled sister. Your young siblings had to carry water from miles away. Neam saw that and he didn't care. He and his mother cooked food and enjoyed eating while your younger sisters and brother starved to death. I don't think it is a good idea to marry a guy like that."

"If you don't want her to get married, then you're responsible for taking care of her siblings!" Grandma screamed.

I shared with them that I wanted to go Thailand to find Mike. Grandma opened her small eyes knowingly.

"See!" she said to Grandpa. "I told you many times that

marriage was the only way to tie her down, but you wouldn't listen—"

I sneaked out of the room and let them blame each other. The group I'd been meeting with decided to go to Thailand in two days. During these two days, many elders, teachers, friends, and others I knew in the village came forward to advise, threaten, beg, question, and try to persuade me to change my mind.

"Leaving a village is not a good idea for a girl, my dear. You will ruin your parents' reputation, which they worked so hard to earn, and you will mess up by doing this," a well-respected elder told me.

"If you've fallen in love with someone else, tell your grand-parents the truth, so you can get married. You don't have to run away with him. You're not using your brain," said a friend of my father.

"Teacher Siv and his wife were a very good couple. I don't understand why they have a daughter who bucks tradition like this," a lady who knew my parents said.

"When a girl leaves the village, the only job she can do to make money is to sell her body as a prostitute," my next-door neighbor commented.

In spite of everything people told me, the next day I asked my grandma to shave my head. This gesture was a sacrifice in exchange for my asking my parents' souls to protect me from danger. In addition, it was good for me not to look attractive.

My brother Ra decided to go with me. I asked my sister Mouch to take care of my younger siblings, because I was not sure if our trip would be safe. In case we didn't make it, my other siblings would survive.

On March 23, 1979, I prepared some rice and other supplies, bent my legs, and bowed my head to the floor in front of my grandparents.

"Grandpa, I would like to say good-bye. Please give me your

blessing." With his eyes full of tears, he gave me his blessing. I turned to my grandma and did the same thing. She exploded, "Go ahead! Go, but never come back to this village!"

My grandmother was a powerful person, but this time she could not stop me. Tears flowing, without saying a word, I pulled my brother Ra's hand and walked out, taking a final look at my sixth sister as she cleaned rice grains in a flat basket.

CHAPTER 15

The Minefield

A TOTAL OF TWENTY-EIGHT ADULTS and children joined the trip to Thailand. The group included a former Buddhist monk, Hok Savann, a middle-aged widower, Mr. Choeun, a former deputy in the Lon Nol government, and his three sons. Another widowed man, Mr. Ry, a former customs officer and general in the military, brought his four orphaned nephews. A bachelor named Oun came with his cousin Pheak and another young man, Hong. One widowed Chinese-Cambodian merchant had four children. Her first daughter, Keav, was also widowed and had a ten-year-old daughter. Her second daughter, Ky, was my former classmate and a good friend. She had a two-year-old daughter. The son, Song, was also a former classmate. The woman's third daughter, Teang, had recently married. She also brought her youngest brother, Koy.

We left on the New Year, April 13, 1979. I wore dark green pants and a black blouse, with a kramar covering my shaved head. In my backpack, I carried a small pot for cooking rice, some rice, and a syringe, left over from the days when my father had used the backpack as his doctor's bag. My brother wore only shorts, with no shirt. Not only our group, but many people, mostly ethnic Chinese who were longtime residents of Cambodia, marched noisily along National Route 5 to the border. We were escaping persecution to pursue freedom. I joined the crowd of refugees without a penny in my pocket.

We all had a common goal: to find a new place to live, to run away from torture and execution, to seek opportunity, and to conquer our fear of the Communist regime. The flow of people walking to the border combined with groups of people who had just been released from the Khmer Rouge zone. People walked in and out of the throng as though it were a festival. They carried all sort of belongings in their oxcarts, in their hand-made push carts, and on bikes. Most people, including my brother and me, walked with bare feet.

We walked twenty to twenty-five kilometers a day, crossing one village and then another. Sometimes we walked alongside flooded rice fields. My eyes would stare at some object on the road for a long time. Once in a while, I saw storks walking with the group, looking for food. Early in the morning, I woke up and cooked rice and packed a lunch so I would not have to spend time at noon. It helped speed up the trip. Before sunset, I looked for someplace close to a village to spend the night; otherwise we would have to sleep on the highway. When sleeping on the road, people took turns guarding each other in case the Khmer Rouge attacked in the middle of the night. I had a long scarf to protect me and my brother from the cold. But the dew that collected through the night made the scarf wet, so the scarf didn't help.

The sky became my house. I waited for the moon and stars to emerge from the darkness, and if they shone, that was my lucky night. When the sky was cloudy, I worried. If it rained in the middle of the night, I had no place to hide. It also meant that I would have to donate more blood to the mosquitoes, which were especially wild on rainy nights. In just a couple of days, my skin was full of rashes from mosquito bites. My poor brother was so skinny, and his feet were blistered from walking so far without shoes. But he never complained.

For several nights, I had the same bad dream. Our journey was a parade that was carrying people to their graves. Suddenly, I saw my mother laughing. She urged me not to continue this trip.

When I woke up, I knew that the trip would be a nightmare for me. But no matter what happened, I would not return home.

A week passed, and my brother and I could not move our legs anymore. His blisters were getting worse. We heard people talking about a train that was going to Battambang. Our group decided to wait for the train so we could rest our feet a little bit. Three days later, the train stopped at the station near where we were staying. Unfortunately, the train was not free. Everyone had to pay to ride—and we had no money.

After wasting three days waiting for the train, I felt hopeless, but we continued the journey. The blisters on my brother's feet were full of dirt, which made his feet ache at night. Sometimes I asked people who had an oxcart if my brother could ride on it.

After twenty-two days, we reached Battambang City, about 100 kilometers from the Thai border. Our group decided to stay for a couple of days to wait for news from the Thai border. But the longer we stayed in the city, the less food we had. My rice supply was dwindling. Other people in the group had gold, which they could use to buy food and other necessities. I knew I could sell my father's syringe for gold. But I did not want to do that.

On the fifth day in Battambang, I was completely out of rice. It was a clear, beautiful morning. I woke up early, pulled the syringe out of my backpack, and looked at it closely. It reminded me of the times my father and I had gone to help a neighbor in the middle of the night. My father had used this syringe to save many lives in the village. Now he was gone, but I still had the syringe. I should take care of it properly. But I needed food and medicine for my brother's feet. I decided to sell the syringe so my brother and I could survive.

～

As soon as I brought it to the market, a man who looked like a nurse offered me one gram of gold. I wanted to change my mind, but the man took the syringe and quickly left. With the gold, I bought rice, medicine, and a good noodle soup for my brother. The next day, we started walking again.

The goal was to reach the Thai border, going through O Chrouv, Koup Nimith, and Nong Chan. We walked for another week and reached the small village of Koup Nimith, on the Thai-Cambodia border. People were going in and out, back and forth, bringing food and supplies from Thailand into Cambodia. Our group stayed overnight in the village, preparing to go to the border the next day. In the village, we heard people talking about robberies, shootings, and other bizarre things that happened while crossing the border. Mr. Choeun asked me to help him hide his 10-karat diamond bracelet. I put it somewhere where no one would find it.

The villagers told my group not to bring our belongings with us. They said that humanitarian organizations would provide us with everything we needed, including clothing, food, and housing, when we reached the refugee camp.

Early the next morning, our group had to wait for more people to head to the Thai border. We were advised to stay close together and travel in a large group to minimize our chance of being robbed. Khmer Rouge guerrillas often ambushed and robbed people at the border.

We walked silently and very fast to get to the camp before sunset. The route to the Thai border traversed thick bamboo fields. The road was muddy, slippery, and dark. The pungent odor of unburied corpses was very bad when the wind blew in our direction. My friend had to give her baby a bit of sleeping pill to calm her down so she would not cry.

We were in the middle of a bamboo field when we heard gunfire 500 meters in front of us. The crowd ran back and people fell down next to each other, screaming "Go back! The Khmer Rouge are coming." I held my brother's hand and looked for shelter. When the guns were silent, people tried to calm down. We continued to walk, staying close to each other.

When we neared the border, some people separated from the crowd and left to join their families who had reached the border before them. Our group stayed together. We were happy because we had reached our goal. I could not wait to see the people from the international agencies, who would welcome us and give us food and clothes. As I was daydreaming, a threatening voice from the nearby bushes called, "Stop!" Everyone stood still. Three Thai men dressed in dark green uniforms and carrying handguns searched us for gold and money. They checked my clothes but found nothing. I was glad I could hide the diamond bracelet for Mr. Choeun. After taking everything of possible value, the three men ran into the bushes. We were free, but sad to have lost our valuables.

Just before sunset on June 10, 1979, our group entered Nong Chan village in Thailand. No one was there to welcome us or give us food. We sat down on the side of the street and tried to cook rice for supper. It was getting dark. The sky clouded over, lightning flashed, and it started to rain. We had no place to go. We had only an old piece of plastic to cover us. The rain poured harder and harder. Water ran down from a field to the place where we were sitting in the street. Everyone got soaked. It rained on and off for about two more hours. As soon as the rain stopped, mosquitoes swarmed on us like flies. My brother and I covered our bodies with wet plastic. We fell asleep in the jellylike mud with no food in our stomachs.

We overslept. Suddenly, I heard a noise, "Pey! Pey! Pey!" and the sound of the hitting sticks that Thai soldiers used. I understood a couple words of Thai. *Pey* meant go. I grabbed my brother's hand and ran toward a place where some other families had taken shelter under a plastic tent. Most of the refugees were Chinese. Some were merchants who were selling food, using Thai currency. I was sad because I did not have any money. Across the street a Red Cross flag hung in front of a small tent, but the workers stood idle, watching all the activity passively.

Our escape group divided up by family to get food from the Red Cross. We helped each other build makeshift shelters. We fell into a rhythm of surviving day to day. During the day, we spent time discussing how to make a case for political asylum and submit it to the United States Embassy. At night, we took turns guarding our tents. We often heard people being robbed and screaming for help. We would wake up and hit an aluminum container to make a loud noise to scare the thief. People did not sleep much because of the commotion from the robberies. The Thai soldiers were very mean. They hit, kicked, and beat refugees for no reason. I was more scared of the Thai soldiers than the Khmer Rouge.

On June 19, the Thai government announced its intention to move all Khmer refugees to In Tam's camp on the Thai-Cambodian border in Preah Vihear province. We had heard a lot about this camp. In Tam was a former officer in the Lon Nol government who had escaped to the United States in 1975. He later established a guerilla military group and set up camps between the Khmer-controlled areas in Cambodia and the Thai border, where his soldiers prepared to fight the Khmer Rouge and gain power in Cambodia. We weren't sure what to do. We thought about going back to Nimith, but it seemed like that would be more dangerous than staying with the group.

On June 22, a Thai military truck full of soldiers arrived at the refugee camp. Soldiers pointed guns at us and forced us onto buses. When one bus filled up, another one would come—dozens of them over the course of five days. People left their belongings behind. Family members were separated. Elders who were sick and could not walk on their own were left in the field, crying and asking for their families. Young children, separated from their parents, sobbed and ran. Behind the long line of people getting on the buses, Thai villagers grabbed merchandise at the refugees' market, put it into their trucks, and left.

Across the street, the Red Cross workers stood and watched

as refugees were forced onto buses. A Red Cross flag still waved above the empty refugee shelter. I realized then that this camp was not recognized by the United Nations High Commissioner on Refugees. I was an illegal refugee.

My group was split up. My brother and I stayed with Hong, Pheak, Oun, and Keav and her daughter. The bus drove day and night, crossing big cities, small towns, villages, farms, forests, and rivers without stopping except for gas and to let us go to the bathroom. At every gas station, Thai women gave us rice, food, and water. I will never forget the eyes of one middle-aged, petite lady with short curly hair who gave me food and water without saying a word. Our group pooled our money and gave it to her. She threw the money back to us in the bus and shook her head. We ate and slept on the bus for two days until we reached a mountain on the Thai-Khmer border.

All the buses were stopped at the border. Thai soldiers let the buses pass one by one. While waiting outside the bus, I was approached by our bus driver. He asked me how many people I had with me. I knew Thai well enough to communicate and understand what was going on. He told me that if I did not want to go back to Cambodia, my brother and I could stay at his friend's house, which was just across the street. He would pick us up when he came back. But I did not think this was a good idea. I didn't know him, didn't speak his language, and didn't know where he would take me. I was afraid that he would sell me as a prostitute. Between staying with him and going to Cambodia, I would rather die in my homeland.

I saw an empty bus coming back across the border. The bus driver moved his finger back and forth across his throat and drove away with a look of terror on his face. I felt hopeless about our chance of surviving. Keav whispered in my ear, "If they send me back to Cambodia, I would rather die on the border. Going back is shameful."

It was my bus's turn to cross the border. The driver called the passengers back onto the bus. Before I boarded, the driver asked me if I had made up my mind. "Thank you for your help, but I cannot accept your offer," I said. I made the decision without regret. The bus took off slowly, heading deep into the jungle. It finally stopped at an unpaved, rough road. I didn't see any houses around. It seemed like a scary place. The trees were very old and tall, and it looked like no one had been here for years.

When we got off the bus, I noticed many personal items, such as shoes, mats, and backpacks all over the place. No one was around. My group did not know where to go. We looked around for a way out. A man dressed in a Thai soldier's uniform walked toward us and spoke in the Khmer language. "Go this way—walk down the hill, and Khmer Serey will welcome you." He pointed down the hill, where I could see some plastic. It looked like a camp. I realized that I was at the top of Dong Reak Mountain in Preah Vihear province.

❧

We did not doubt that there was a camp run by In Tam. All of us struggled without hesitation to reach the destination. A few yards from me, a child cried for water. I saw a Thai soldier come out of the bushes, open his bottle, give the child water, and leave without saying a word.

The hill was a steep cliff. We climbed down by holding onto tree roots or branches. As we climbed down, the Thai soldiers asked us for our Thai money, telling us that we could not spend it here.

After a couple hundred yards, I saw some people who had come from the same camp in Nong Chan where we'd been. Mr. Choeun saw his neighbor, who had just delivered a baby by herself. She was waiting for her husband, who had gone down to the valley to bring water for her. Mr. Choeun asked her why nobody made a move to leave this place. "There are a ton of mines everywhere," she said. As they talked, the sound of a mine explosion vibrated through the jungle. Horrified people screamed for help. I felt that this was it—a dead end. Keav kept repeating into my ear that she rather would rather die than return home.

We continued our descent to the bottom of the hill. About 200 feet from the bottom, while holding a tree root that looked like a rope, I saw men in a line pulling the root upward to the top of the mountain. I felt confused about what was going on down there. Fifteen minutes later, gunfire from the top of the mountain shot toward these men. One by one, they dropped to the ground like rocks. When their bodies hit the ground, they touched mines, and the sound of explosions mingled with screaming and weeping. But I still wanted to see what was going on at the bottom of the hill.

Finally, my group reached the destination. We discovered that there was no guerilla camp. Instead, we found all the refugees from Nong Chan camped in a minefield. They were miserable, sitting in the bushes, abandoned there with no food or water. Many dead bodies, young and old, smelled of blood. I looked in my brother's eyes, regretful that I had brought him along. "Welcome to hell," I whispered.

We sat down on a little hill, waiting for word from Mr. Ry, the former general in the Lon Nol regime. We were warned by many people not to walk around. Several places around us were covered by tree branches, leaves, old clothes, or paper, as a warning of where the mines were. I had never seen a mine in my life. They were planted in the ground about four to five feet apart. Only the red head like a match showed clearly on top of the mine, which was about the size of a can of sardines. I wondered who had set up this land mine. The Khmer Rouge or the Thai soldiers? No one could give me an answer. At this point, an answer wouldn't help anyway . . . the solution was to get out.

Everyone was so hungry. We ate raw instant noodles. My friend's daughter cried for water. There was no water. I sat beside Ra watching some people burn something. Behind me, Keav expressed her disappointment. Fifteen yards in front of me, a seven-year-old girl wandered around looking for wood. An old man screamed, "Stop! There's a mine right there!" The mine exploded as he spoke. The sound almost broke my eardrum. At the same time, I felt hot steam pass over my face like steam from boiling water. A man's voice yelled to calm down the crowd: "Stay where you are, don't move. There are still many mines around you."

When I opened my eyes, I saw blood all over my body and Ra's body. We cried and hugged each other, believing that we would die soon. I admitted to my brother that I had made a mistake in bringing him here, and I was sorry if something happened to him. "If I die, please find a way out of here," I sobbed. I used my bloody hand to wipe my tears. I checked my body and Ra's quickly to be sure we were all right. We were covered in blood, but we had no pain.

We stopped crying and tried to see what was going on. Some of our group members were injured, but not very seriously. A little girl cried behind my back. As I turned toward her, I saw Keav fall to the ground with her eyes open. Blood, flowing like water, soaked the left side of her head. A sharp cut the width of a finger crossed her left breast into the middle of her chest. Her daughter, Peov, held Keav's head and cried for help. Keav's mother called, "Keav! Keav! Keav! Do you hear me?" but there was no answer. Her family members decided to carry her out to save her life. I felt so sorry for her daughter. I wondered why the mine explosion had to hurt Keav. She was sitting behind me. It should have been me, not her.

After her family left, our group decided to get out of this hell. We had no choice. If we got out, we might have a chance to live, rather than being killed by a mine explosion. Our group took a chance and followed a person who called himself a guide.

"If you want to get out, you must listen to me," the guide said. "There are many mines, as you can see. If you hear another mine explosion, stay still . . . don't move . . . try to remain calm." As we started to walk, I told my brother to stay behind me.

"Be careful! There's a mine near your right foot. I put a tree branch over it," the guide warned us. On the way out, while waiting for our orders, I saw people who had just been killed by the mines. Their bodies lay on the ground with their heads chopped off and legs and arms severed. Blood flowing on the ground smelled like fish. The 110° temperature made the bodies rot quickly. One survivor who had lost her legs sat sobbing and dug in the ground with a tree branch to cover the corpses. She begged us to take her out: "Please take me along with you. I'll do anything for you, I'll never forget your kindness. Please—I will give you money or gold." No one paid attention to her. Money did not make any sense anymore. Life and death were more important than anything else. Not far from the woman without legs, a baby about six or seven months old still sucked her dead mother's breast.

∾

"Stay right there, don't move," the guide ordered. "Wait until the person in front of you crosses the big rock first. There's a mine under that rock." I swallowed very hard in my empty throat and held my breath. While waiting my turn, I saw a man's body face down holding a kettle full of blood under his chest. "Oh God! His wife was at the top of the hill. She had a baby and was waiting for him to carry water to her!" Mr. Choeun exclaimed.

∾

It was my turn to cross the big rock. As I walked over it, I looked down and saw the mine clearly. It looked exactly like a battery. Next to the big rock was the body of a woman who had died at least a couple of days ago. Maggots crawled all over the corpse. She held her baby, also dead, in front of her and had a backpack full of brand-new sarongs. Under the pack of sarongs, I saw a

mine. I wondered who had put all these mines here to kill innocent people. I did not understand why the Thai soldiers had sent
the refugees here. Another mine exploded about twenty yards
from where I was. Again there was screaming, crying, and yelling
for help. That explosion took another ten or twenty lives.

It took my group about two hours to walk approximately 100
feet. My dry throat almost killed me and my stomach was crawling for food. My brother and I had not had water or food for almost a day. I looked at my brother's face. He was very quiet and
very tired. I could not wait to get out of this hell, so I could cook
for us. We passed another limbless man who could not get out
of the bushes. "Watch your step, there's another mine to your
right," the guide warned us.

Another two hours passed. Thanks to the guide, our group
got out of the minefield successfully. After reaching the safe place,
I ran toward a small pond. I submerged my mouth into the water
to drink. I swallowed as much water as I could until a small crea-
ture crawled into my mouth. Near the pond lay the corpse of a
man who'd been dead about a week. I stood up and looked at the
dead body with a horrible taste in my mouth.

We got out of that hell before sunset. We walked across the
valley while mines continued to explode not far from us. Another
half hour later, we reached the road that went from the mountains of Thailand into Cambodia. There, I saw sister Keav's
daughter, Peov, sitting near her mother's grave. I kneeled in front
of the grave and prayed: "May your body and soul rest in peace,
and may you help take care of your daughter and help me to have
a safe trip." Keav was the only member of our group whom we
lost. It was very sad for her daughter.

I stood and looked back toward the minefield and prayed for
all the poor people stuck there without any help. In a Cambodian funeral, special music is played on traditional instru-
ments. In the jungle, people didn't have that comfort. Instead,
the sound of the cicadas singing in various tones and the rustle

of the wind gently blowing the leaves created the music to accompany the burying of the dead and the mourning of the surviving family.

I had thought that living under the Communist regime had given me enough pain and suffering, but the minefield experience was worse. It was a clear picture of hell and death. I had to face my own death, and this near-miss gave me strength to live, hope for the future, and an appreciation for what I still had. Even as I write this story, I still think about the lady with the broken leg and the baby who sucked his dead mother's breast.

CHAPTER 16

Temporary Respite

PREAH VIHEAR PROVINCE was a sparsely populated region of rain forests. Many minority groups, such as the Kouy, Steang, and Pnorng, lived there. They hunted, picked fruit, and planted potatoes and corn. They spoke their own language, so we could not communicate with them.

I had reached a dead end. It didn't make sense to return to Pursat Province. Where should I go? There was no answer. I took life one day at a time. For now, I stayed with the group of refugees. I would think about where to go next when I reached Kompong Thom.

After getting out of the minefield, we faced a new problem: lack of food. Our supply of rice was limited. Along the way to our new destination, Vietnamese soldiers offered us some potato flour to make bread. Sometimes I walked all day long without seeing any villagers. It was dangerous to sleep along the road because we saw many tiger claws and elephant feet. The refugees had to stick together and build a fire in the middle of the group to protect each other from wild animals.

About a week later, I heard on the Voice of America in a villager's house that a humanitarian organization had come to rescue the refugees who were left behind in the minefield, Phnom Dang Rag. These people would have a new home in the United States. "They deserve that," I thought.

It was getting harder to find food. The group decided to split apart and travel in families. My brother and I did not have many problems because I was outgoing and connected easily with the villagers we met. They shared whatever they had with us, such as dried salted rabbit, venison, elephant meat, smoked boar, and potatoes. Some families even offered me a place to live.

∾

We walked up to thirty kilometers a day across the jungle, with no water. In the Kouy village, the people did not have any clothes on. When we asked for water, they threatened us with bows and arrows. We had to run for another mile just to find water. Some days, we managed only a couple of kilometers because villagers alerted us that the Khmer Rouge might ambush refugees in the jungle.

We traveled through more than ten villages and finally reached Kompong Thom Province. At a large school shelter, Vietnamese soldiers distributed rice to refugees. I had rice, but no wood to cook it. Speaking Vietnamese, I asked a soldier for wood. He gave me a whole bunch of wood, and that night he brought me more rice. I felt embarrassed that he thought I could speak Vietnamese. Actually, I spoke only a little, enough to communicate with him. I told him that my parents were killed in the Communist regime. The second night, he brought me more rice, which made the other refugees jealous. They told my brother that the soldier was in love with me and I would go off to Saigon with him and leave my brother on his own.

Mr. Choeun's family and Mr. Neorng's family decided to go to Battambang Province. Mr. Ry planned to go back to Phnom Penh. All the families from our group would leave the next day. I didn't know where to go. I did not know anyone in Battambang or Phnom Penh. Only Hong, Pheak, Ra, and I were undecided about where to go. That night, I heard a family next to me talking about a village in Kompong Cham Province called Bosknor. Bosknor had excellent farmland. People could survive there without rice. There were plenty of bananas, bamboo, potatoes, and other vegetables all year round.

✺

On the third day, early in the morning, one by one each family prepared to leave Kompong Thom. Ra announced he would go with one of the families. He believed that I was planning to marry the Vietnamese soldier and leave him behind. I didn't know how to explain to him so he would understand me. I stood in front of the house and watched him walk away from me. I feared that I would never see him again, that I'd lost him. But if he did not trust me and he believed other people more than his own sister, then that was it. Overwhelmed and angry, I walked back into the house. I heard footsteps and a loud cry. Mr. Neorng brought my brother back. "You're crazy, you should stay with your sister," he told Ra. "No one else will care for you like your own sister. . . . Go to her!" I was happy to see my brother back, but disappointed that he had believed an outsider.

Hong, Pheak, Ra, and I were left in the big empty house. We decided to go to Bosknor, a place we had never been. We walked along the National Route and saw a group of people waiting for a truck heading to Kompong Cham Province. We asked the truck driver for a ride, and he demanded gold. I handed him a piece of the gold I'd gotten from selling my father's syringe. It was all I had left. The driver let all four of us sit in the truck, then put in a full load of items and a plastic cover over us. We arrived at Kompong Cham City in the afternoon.

People in the city were very rude. They looked at us like we were bad people. It wasn't easy to ask them for food. Without food or gold, what could we do? We sat on a bench and tried to figure out a way to survive for a couple of days in the city. Most of the people we saw wanted to rob us rather than help. We looked at each other in despair. Pheak moved her diamond ring back and forth on her finger. "This is the ring that my mother gave me before she passed away," she said tearfully. "The only way we can survive is if I sell it." I felt sorry that she had to do this for my brother and me.

Merchants were not interested in buying diamonds, however. They wanted gold, only gold. No one wanted to buy Pheak's ring. Finally, the only choice she had was to exchange the ring for ten cans of rice. A little way outside the city, we met a family with a small house. We asked if we could stay overnight. The woman agreed and told us how to get to Bosknor.

Early the next morning, we started out on foot to Bosknor, which was about fifteen kilometers from Kompong Cham. We asked a truck driver who was on his way to Kompong Thom to take us as far as Bosknor. This time the driver did not demand gold. When we got to Bosknor, we met a man who suggested that we see the *Choav Sang Kat,* the villager-in-charge. We took his advice and tried to come up with a story so the man in charge would let us stay in the village.

When we found the villager-in-charge, Mr. Son, we paid him our respects. He was a short man of about fifty-five, with curly hair. I told him that Hong, Ra, and I were siblings and Pheak was our cousin. We had been separated from our parents at Battambang and believed they were sent to this village. Mr. Son gasped and said, "I don't think your parents survived here. All New People were executed before the Vietnamese invasion." He asked us where we were going next. We had no answer. Then he asked, "How much education do you have? The village is looking for a teacher." We discussed it and accepted his offer. The job would pay fifteen cans of rice and twenty cans of corn per month. So with Hong and I both teaching, we would get thirty cans of rice and forty cans of corn a month.

∽

Mr. Son offered to let us live in the empty house of his neighbor, who had gone to work in the city for a while. He gave us a small rice field to plant rice and showed us where to look for bananas, bamboo shoots, potatoes, and vegetables. We were so happy.

For a week, I had a high fever, running a temperature of 104 to 105 day and night. Hong found herbs and smashed them with coconut juice and gave me the mixture to drink. He was like a brother to me. His medicine helped cool down my fever, but only for an hour or so. Then my temperature rose again. I could not eat or drink for a week. I had nightmares every night. I dreamed that my mother's spirit wanted me to go home. She was very angry and asked my father to slap me hard. The next day when I woke up, I decided to fight back by blaming her for not letting me go to the United States with Mike. From then on, my fever got better, but my hair started to fall out like I was a cancer patient.

Hong and I taught students in the morning, then looked for fruits and vegetables in the afternoon with my brother. We found graves the size of small ponds where the Khmer Rouge had buried civilians before the Vietnamese invasion. Each grave contained fifty to eighty people. Their bodies still looked fresh, and they were wearing clothes. Some corpses had ropes tying their hands behind their back. Some had a hole in their skull.

Time flew by . . . four month passed. We made friends in the village. Pheak and Hong became closer and closer, falling in love. I was happy for them.

My own goal of reaching the Thai border and escaping to freedom was still in my mind. I never gave up this hope. One day, I saw that my neighbor had brought some things back from the Thai border. He told me there were camps at the border again. Many refugees had gone to the United States, Australia, France, and other countries.

At the same time, Mr. Son and his wife gave me the option of marrying a guy in the village, so my life would settle down. Mr. Son would even help us cut trees to build a house.

✤

I discussed the trip to Thailand again with Hong and Pheak. They wanted to stay in Bosknor and build a life together, along with the baby that was on the way.

I told Mr. Son the truth about myself and thanked him for all his help. He told me stories he'd heard about Thai soldiers who raped women and sold them into prostitution. He warned me of the many dangers in Thailand. I believed him and accepted that these were facts. But nothing could not diminish my determination to pursue my goal.

When I told my brother that we would be leaving soon, he looked into my eyes. "I don't want to go. I'm so afraid of mine explosions," he said. "How about if we just live here?"

"We left our village to get out of Cambodia. We're still in Cambodia. As long as I have not reached our goal, I will not give up," I explained. "We have to go, brother! Please just try one more time."

CHAPTER 17

The Second Escape To Thailand

THE NIGHT BEFORE WE WERE TO LEAVE for the Thai border, I packed and got ready so we could set out early in the morning. In my backpack I had some rice, a small pot for cooking, and a couple packs of cigarettes. I looked at my long pants, which had gotten shorter and shorter and were covered with patches. I stayed up late that night talking with Hong and Pheak. Before I fell asleep, I prayed to my father to let me know that my trip would be successful by sending me a good dream. I dreamed about big tall buildings full of a beautiful light at night. I had never seen such buildings and lights in my life. In the dream, my father gave me a gold necklace to take with me on my trip. I woke up around three A.M. and thought that the dream was lucky.

I left Bosknor while the villagers still slept. I was thankful to Mr. Son, whom I considered a brother, and to my students and the other people I'd met.

We reached Chamkar Leu, about twenty-five kilometers from Bosknor. We crossed a rubber field, a very dark, very quiet, very scary place. Once in a while I saw a group of bicyclists coming from the opposite direction with a full load of items from Thailand. My brother and I stopped at a crossroads. It was hard to figure out which way to go. We stood there for a little while and looked around. Nearby, an old man walked his bicycle, which had a flat tire. "Do you know where you are going?" he asked me gently.

"We want to go to Barraay Teak Tlar, and I don't know which road to take!" I answered promptly.

"Follow me," he said, pointing out the way to me.

As we walked, he said, "Last week, Khmer Rouge soldiers set up a roadblock and arrested two women who were riding their bicycles home. They cut their bodies in half and threw them a couple yards from here." His story gave me goosebumps, and I thought I was lucky that he had showed me the right way out. It took us about an hour to cross the rubber field. The old man said good-bye and left.

On the road, a middle-aged man rode his oxcart with a young man behind. The young man looked at my brother's skinny legs with pity. He grabbed my brother to ride on the oxcart while his father asked me where I was going. "I'm looking for my aunt in Kompong Thom," I said.

"You look very tired," the man said. "Would you like to stop at my house to rest for a while? How about it?" he offered sincerely. I was always wary of free offers, but I decided to trust him.

At his home, he cooked rice and made a chicken soup. I had not eaten that kind of food for so long. He prepared the meal while his son took care of the cows. He encouraged me to bathe at the well by his house. I cleaned my feet and hands instead, since I didn't have any clothes to change into. At the well, a lady was washing her clothes. She asked, "Are you related to that house owner?"

"No," I answered.

"Do you know that he's looking for a wife for his son? His son is very nice, but the man's wife is cheap and mean."

I knew I had to prepare an answer for the old man. At lunchtime, the old man, his son, Ra, and I sat on the mat in a circle around the rice and the chicken soup, which were delicious.

"You are a beautiful girl," the man began. "It is dangerous for you to walk like this. Stay with me. I can take care of you. I have plenty of rice to feed you," he continued while his son smiled at me. How could he see my beauty? I had lost almost all my hair. I was so skinny and ugly. "Yes, Uncle, but I want to find my aunt in Kompong Thom first. If I can't find her, I will come back to stay with you."

After the delicious lunch, I said good-bye to the two men. My brother and I had more energy than before. We made it to the National Route at Barraay Teak Tlar before sunset. We were worried, because we weren't sure where we could sleep that would be safe. We kept walking while an old truck drove by us very fast. A couple of minutes later, we heard the truck blow out a tire, a sound like a mine explosion.

The truck driver stopped at the side of the road to fix the flat tire. I begged the young man to let us ride in his truck. He said there was no space to sit. I begged him again and again. He still refused. I didn't know what to do. A woman standing near me told me to offer him a cigarette. I went to the driver again. "I'll sit on the floor, on racks, on bags, on whatever you have, as long as my brother and I can get in the truck . . . I'll go wherever you're going . . . I'll give you cigarettes." I said anything I could think of until he could not refuse. He agreed to let my brother and I get in the truck. After he finished repairing the tire, the truck driver took a swig from a bottle of alcohol.

The truck was as old as my grandparents. The driver pushed Ra and me into the back. Inside it was very dark. At first, I thought the truck was empty. But as the driver pushed me in, I fell onto another body, and someone screamed from the back, "I told you no more people, did you hear what I told you? Why do you keep picking up strangers?" The driver pretended not to hear what the lady said to him. He told me his story, how he had fought the Vietnamese soldiers and how he was in love with a beautiful Vietnamese girl. He talked nonstop. I thought he was drunk.

Inside the truck, the temperature was about 110, but it was better than walking. As my eyes adjusted to the dark, I saw more people in the truck. The truck was half full of rice bags. On top of the rice bags were twenty to thirty people, ranging in age from seventy-five to a month-old baby. Everyone was very quiet except the woman who had yelled at the truck driver. "How much gold did you pay the driver?" a lady whispered in my ear. "How much did you pay him?" I asked back. "Two Chi," she answered. (Chi is a measure of gold equal to about ¼ ounce.) "I gave him two packs of cigarettes," I said. "That's not fair!" she screamed. "You misunderstand—I paid him two packs of cigarette and dollars," I said. The word *dollars* shut the lady up.

"Oh no, we have a problem," the driver screamed. "We may need to push the truck because the bridge is broken." "No!" everyone yelled. The driver used his flashlight to inspect the bridge. Through a small hole in the side of the truck, I could see a lake below us. "There are two flat boards, one on each side. I'll try to pass over the lake on these. It if works, fine, but if not, we'll fall into the water. Do you hear me?" I started to pray like the other passengers. I worried about how the drunk driver could stay on the boards without falling.

He stopped in the middle of the bridge. We heard a cracking sound. Then the truck moved slowly forward. I could feel the bridge vibrating underneath us. The truck was stuck at the end of the bridge. The driver moved slowly, pushing back and forth. Finally, he made it across. Everyone breathed in relief.

The truck reached Kompong Thom City at midnight. My brother and I slept in the truck because we were afraid the driver would leave without us the next day.

The driver overslept from drinking too much. At nine A.M., I gave him two packs of cigarettes and asked to continue with him. His next stop would be Siem Reap Province. I was lucky. The ride saved us a lot of time.

It took the truck a whole day to get to Siem Reap City.

Everyone got out of the truck and looked for a place to sleep. We asked the owner of a big house near the market if we could sleep under the house. Then I cooked for me and Ra. That night, the families from the truck got together and discussed how to get to Svay Sisophon in Battambang Province. These people were all trying to make it to Thailand too. They had a lot of gold, so they decided to pool their money to hire a guide to reach the border. The group needed two ounces of gold from each family. I told them honestly that I had no gold.

On of the men said, "I swore I would never travel with people who were broke, because they just suck other people's blood." I was sad but said nothing. This man did not understand my life. I did not need his money.

I wanted to see if there was any chance of finding a truck that was going to Battambang. But I heard a lot of scary stories about robberies, shootings, and rapes that happened on the long trip to Battambang. No one walked the route from Siem Reap to Battambang. I would have to try to go by truck. I believed that God would not close the door on me.

I waited for a truck until the afternoon. Then I found out that no trucks were allowed to go that way. I decided to walk to Battambang. Another woman wanted to join me and my brother. I appreciated having her with us. She introduced herself as Khom. She was about five foot three, with dark skin and curly hair. She was very quiet and looked sad. Like me, she did not have enough gold to pay for the guide.

Khom had been to Norg Samith Camp with her husband. Unfortunately, he ran away with another woman. I helped her carry her things. She could hardly talk. She seemed very depressed. After walking about thirteen kilometers from Siem Reap, we were hungry. We started to cook supper. I let my brother cook the rice while I took two cans of rice to exchange for dried fish at a small grocery nearby.

At the grocery, I saw a woman telling a fortune for another

customer. After she finished, she asked me if I wanted to know my future. It would cost one can of rice. I looked at the two cans and thought about it. "Yes," I said. She showed me the tarot cards and asked me to choose three.

"Well," she said, "the cards say that you have two other people with you. But be careful about a dark-skinned woman who is with you. She is not very kind.

"You will make a long trip, which will bring fortune and luck. Keep walking to your left. You will find kind people to rescue you. There will be men who are in love with you." She chuckled. "Oh, I see good fortune for you, very, very good." I gave her a can of rice. With the other can of rice, I bought a small bowl of sour soup.

I had never believed fortune tellers before. But this time, I wondered how she knew about the dark-skinned woman who was with me. How did she know that I had a long trip ahead? Who was going to fall in love with a poor ugly girl like me? Maybe I would walk toward the left to see if her predictions would come true.

After supper, my brother, Khom, and I started to walk again, staying on the left-hand side of the road, as the fortune teller had told me. Before sunset, we walked about two kilometers. The road was very quiet. No one came by in cars, trucks, or on bikes. Walking about two more kilometers, I saw five bicyclists coming toward us. One of the men stopped and asked me, "Where are you going? "

"To Battambang," I answered.

"We're going there too. But one of the villagers told us that if we could not reach another village before sunset, we shouldn't take the risk of stopping on the road because soldiers wait to rob travelers, especially girls. That's why we're coming back."

"Thank you for telling me," I said. "But I have no way back to Siem Reap." I looked at him hopelessly as I took a deep breath and continued to walk.

"Hey!" the man called. "We can take you back to Siem Reap, and in the morning we can take you to Battambang. How about it?"

I looked at all five bicyclists one by one. They seemed trustworthy. I talked with Khom about the plan. She agreed.

We all went back to Siem Reap. I rode with a man named Tha. He explained that his group was from Kompong Cham Province. We shared our stories with each other. My life story moved him deeply. But we lived in two different worlds. He was married and had a six-month-old baby. I had my goal of escaping the persecution in Cambodia. He felt bad that he had not met me when he was single. I told him that that was the will of God. Tha said that he had served as one of Pol Pot's soldiers. He was forced to become a soldier while visiting his parents in the Khmer Rouge zone when he was in ninth grade. Tha was a respectful gentleman with a good heart.

We reached Siem Reap after sunset. The five men even offered us some of their food. I was very thankful for their kindness. I was especially happy to see my brother riding on a bicycle instead of walking on bare feet.

The next morning, we ran into another setback. Travel still required an official letter of permission signed by a deputy of each province. We were stuck because we had no permission letter to go to Battambang Province. Ten minutes later, we heard that a group of people from Battambang wanted to travel to Kompong Cham. We were an excellent match. Our two groups exchanged permission letters. At 10:00 A.M, our group took off toward Battambang.

Our bicyclists passed through one village after another. The road between the villages was very quiet and scary, bordered only by acres of rice fields. I saw a couple of unburied corpses along the road.

The men peddled all day long. We knew we would not make it to Svay Sisophon before sunset, but we were trying to reach the next village on the road. About ten kilometers from the village, we saw many bicyclists stopped by a roadblock. Three Vietnamese soldiers holding guns sat at the side of the road, and a tree branch blocked the route. Tha asked one of the bicyclists, "What's going on?"

"The Vietnamese soldiers want to rob us. They're waiting for sunset," the old man whispered.

We all looked at each other with no solution. Among the forty travelers were only two women, Khom and I. "Has anyone talked with the soldiers and offered them something?" Tha asked.

"They refused," the man answered.

Our frustration escalated. Many of the travelers were restless and anxious because they had gold with them. Tha and Seng came to me and said, "People have been begging the soldiers to let us through, but they refused. You're the only one who can communicate with them."

"Me! No way! Do you think I am bait to catch these soldiers? Why me? Why not Khom?" I frowned. Tha looked at me intently. "I believe that you are the only one who can do this," he said. "I don't think you'll let the soldiers rob us. Look, the sun is setting now. If it gets dark we're all in big trouble. Please, just try."

I said, "Give me a couple of seconds, but if something happens to me, you're responsible for taking care of my brother, OK?"

I had no idea what I was doing. As I walked toward the three soldiers, a hundred eyes watched me. I spoke to the soldiers in Vietnamese. "Hi! How are you, brothers?"

"I am fine, and you?" one of the men answered.

"Actually, brothers, I just had a baby about three months ago. I left my baby with a neighbor while I went to Siem Reap to look for rice and food. Because my parents were Vietnamese, the Khmer Rouge killed them, brothers." I looked down and pretended that I was crying.

"Really! Your parents were killed by the Khmer Rouge?"

"Yes! Brothers, my husband was also killed before you came to save us. Please let me and my friends go. We are survivors. If you do not pity me, think about my little baby who I left a couple of days ago with the neighbor, without milk. He will cry and suffer without me ... please let me go. I think my group can offer you many packages of cigarettes."

"All right, all right!" the soldier replied. Behind me, Tha alerted the travelers to give their cigarettes to the soldiers. Everyone was so grateful for my negotiation.

We reached the village after sunset. We stayed overnight at the main kitchen there. I cooked for the bicyclists and we ate together. Tha and I had a long talk that night. I don't recall what we talked about, but one thing I do remember was a comment he made about me. He said because I was so smart, he would not be a good match for me even if he were single. He trusted that I would find my way to a new country without any difficulty and that I would find the right partner in the future.

The next morning, we headed to Svay Sisophon without any problems. After five hours on the bikes, we reached our destination around noon. Tha's group had relatives in Sisophon and stayed with them while they bought things in Sisophon to take back to Kompong Cham. They shopped in the afternoon so they could leave early the next morning.

My brother, Khom, and I slept in an open booth at the market, a couple of blocks from Tha's family. Tha and I talked until midnight, when we were interrupted by a heavy rain. That night the rain poured from the sky and the thunder and lightning threatened.

In spite of the heavy rain and no blanket, we slept through the night to help our bodies rest so we would have enough energy to continue our trip the next morning.

CHAPTER 18

At The Border

AT THE END OF DECEMBER 1979, Ra, Khom, and I said good-bye to Tha and his group. Tha had a sad face. He gave me a gram of gold that he had left after shopping. We all had to leave to continue a journey in which we did not know what was going to happen to us.

A lot of families were making the trip to the Thai border. About three kilometers outside Svay Sisophon, the road was blocked by Vietnamese soldiers. More than a hundred people were stopped there. While the crowed milled around, two trucks drove past. My brother, Khom, and I seized the opportunity and ran alongside the trucks so the soldiers would not see us.

We ran for a while, far enough to get past the Vietnamese soldiers. We walked about another kilometer, then heard screaming in the bushes ahead of us. "Robbery!" a man screamed. Everyone was quiet and hid in the bushes.

Khom was exhausted and could no longer carry her belongings. I helped her with them. The road was slippery because of the heavy rain the night before, and Khom's bag was also heavy. I fell into the mud many times. Suddenly, gunfire from the bushes ahead of us shot in our direction. Everyone ran for shelter. My brother and I had experience and knew to get down on the ground right away. About half an hour later, it was quiet. The flow of people continued walking again.

We entered the Nong Samith camp at the border around

noon. Khom asked for her belongings back. I followed the people ahead of us. Next to me was my brother. Khom walked behind us. The people who walked with us were welcomed by relatives and friends. In the camp, there were many plastic tents in rows with an outdoor kitchen. Wet clothes hung outside the shelters. The children running around looked healthier than those in the village. At noon refugees and soldiers' wives cooked food and ate together. My stomach crawled because of the smell. My brother swallowed his saliva to quell the weird sound in his stomach.

While observing all of this, we lost Khom. I called her name and looked for her everywhere. No one seemed to have seen her. She just disappeared in a moment. I had trusted her to show me where to go for help or to find a place to stay for at least a night. Now she had vanished.

My brother looked tired and very hungry. I had no rice left to cook. Why had Khom left me like this? I did not understand. I had helped carry her heavy bags from Siem Reap to the camp. "Well, I hope that God will not close the door on me," I whispered. I asked a woman about resources in the camp. "If you are a new arrival, go down to the administration office," she told me. "They'll give you rice and food. They will also register you and help you find a place to stay."

"Thank you very much," I said. "May my brother stay with you while I go down to the office?" She agreed and I assured Ra I would be back soon.

I walked toward the Sangkat office and joined a long line of other refugees waiting to get rice. While waiting, I looked for people I might know who could give me a hand. On a bulletin board I saw notices from people who had recently arrived in such places as the United States, France, Australia, and New Zealand who were looking for their relatives. So it was true that some people made it to "the third country."

At the registration desk, a woman with short curly hair wrote my name on the list without lifting her face. When she asked me questions about my family, she looked up. I said, "Borin! Do you remember me?"

"You look familiar but I can't recall who you are," she said. She tried to place me. Ashamed of how I looked, I pulled my kramar from my shaved head. My voice jogged her memory. "You're Darina, aren't you?"

" Yes," I answered. "I just got here a couple hours ago. I'm so hungry—I have nothing to eat." I said bluntly.

"Oh, you can stay with me for a while. Here's my address—I'm off work at 4:30. I'll see you there."

"All right, I'll go get my brother. Thank you very much!"

I ran back as fast as I could to get my brother. At the place where I'd left him, I did not see Ra or the woman. Panicked, I looked all around the area. If I could not find him, there was no sense in my living. I sat down near the tree where I last saw him, cried, and prayed for his return.

Two small hands suddenly touched my face while my tears dripped down. "It's me, Ra," my brother yelled. I immediately stopped crying and faced him. "God! You scared me, where did you go?" I asked.

"That woman gave me some rice and soup. It tasted so good. Then I went to take a shower near the well over there," he explained.

I thanked the woman who had given my brother a good lunch, and we went off to find my friend's house. She lived in a small hut with four other people. Tonight, there would be seven people sleeping in it.

Life in the camp was not easy. I needed money for more food. I asked Borin how I could get a job so I could feed my family. She told about another one of my classmates, Sarath, who worked at a grocery and might need help. The next morning, I went straight to find her. "Sarath, do you remember me?" I asked. "Yes, how are you?" she said in a low voice. She did not seem surprised to see me. "I'm fine, and you?" I tried to lower my voice as well. "I'm broke. My husband left me for another woman," she said. I felt it was no use to ask her if I could help sell groceries. I said good-bye and left feeling hopeless. How would I make money to support myself? I could look for a job with a humanitarian organization, but I had spoken English for four years.

From the middle of nowhere, I saw an American man dressed in a gray shirt and khaki pants. He had black hair and a beard. I thought about Mike right away when I saw him. "Hello sir, how are you?" I asked him. I believed that if I found Mike, he would surely help me.

"I'm fine, thank you, and you?"

"So-so," I answered. I did not expect him to engage in conversation. I was just being polite to a foreigner.

"My name is David James," he said. "How long have you been here?"

"I'm Darina. I have been here about two days," I spoke very slowly to practice my abandoned English. "Do know my friend Michael Inghim? He worked for the United States embassy in Cambodia in 1975."

"No," he answered. "There were many Americans in Cambodia in 1975."

"Yes, you're right." I switched the subject. "I'm looking for a job, but can't find anything. Can you help me?" I didn't waste any time getting to the point.

"If you go to the Khoa I Dang camp, I can help you get work with CARE, but around here, I can't help you. Here's my business card. If you get to Khoa I Dang camp, send me a letter, OK?" he explained.

"Thank you very much," I answered.

On his business card, it said that David James was a psychologist. He worked for CARE in Bangkok. I asked my friend Borin about the Khoa I Dang camp. She told me the camp was in Thai territory. A truck from there came to pick up refugees every morning. I asked her why she didn't want to go to Khoa I Dang.

She told me about problems with the Thai soldiers and joked about poison in the water and other scary stories. But I wanted to go there. I planned to go as soon as possible.

∾

January 8, 1980, was a beautiful sunny day in the Nong Samith camp. People were working hard to feed their families, doing whatever it took, smuggling items from Thai villages or selling food or laboring, and doing their chores as usual. I was trying to get in to talk with an American medical doctor to ask for a job. The Khmer worker at the clinic would not allow me to talk with him, however.

I pretended that I was sick. When it was my turn to see the doctor, I talked with him in English without an interpreter. The conversation flowed very well. Suddenly, rockets flew over our heads and exploded just a couple of blocks away. Guerilla troops were fighting. Everyone ducked to the ground while the foreign doctors and volunteers ran to their trucks. Instead of diving to the ground, I stood there and looked at the many trucks that were transporting the foreigners out of the danger zone. How lucky they were to escape by truck. I thought of our bad luck to born as Cambodians.

I felt miserable as I walked toward my friend's hut to look for Ra, who was probably scared to death without me there. The bombs exploded and many shells dropped. The gunfire sounded like popcorn popping. Refugees ran in different directions. In front of me a four-year-old boy fell. A mother carried her baby and dragged another child into a hole in the ground that had been dug to hold water. Everyone screamed and yelled for help. I ran in the opposite direction of the refugees. They bumped and pushed me.

I did not care if a bomb or shell hit or killed me. My life was miserable anyway. I found my brother at Borin's hut, crying and looking for me. All my friends and neighbors had left.

Ra ran up to me and pulled my hand. We joined many other refugees who were fleeing into Thailand.

The shells, bombs, and bullets were chasing us. I could feel the reverberations at my back. Ra stumbled and fell to the ground. I picked him up while bullets flew past my ears with a frightening sound. I saw that there was a long line of refugees waiting to board trucks. One full truck left and another filled up. I did not know for sure where these trucks were heading. My brother and I looked at each other suspiciously. I did not want to find myself in a minefield for a second time. As I stood there trying to think rationally, a voice behind me yelled, "Get into the truck! Go!" A woman pushed me out of the way and said, "Go, dummy—to another camp."

On the main road, I saw a UNHCR pickup truck with the UN flag flying in front. I felt confident that it would be safe for my brother and me to get on this truck.

CHAPTER 19

Refugee Camp

MY BROTHER AND I SMILED at each other for the first time during our long, difficult journey. We hoped we had come to the right place, a safe place. The truck, loaded with refugees, passed through a big gate with a sign that said "Khoa I Dang Camp" and a UNHCR flag. The truck dropped us inside.

The UNHCR flag assured me that the camp was an official refugee camp, and we would be protected from what had happened to us at Nong Chan. This camp was located near a mountain called Khoa I Dang. Long rows of huts were set up for the refugees. Some huts had blue plastic roofs, while others were made of palm leaves. A couple of silver water tanks stood in front of the shelters, and there were outdoor toilets behind the huts. The camp also had makeshift hospitals.

Many refugees were standing around and looking for their friends and relatives. Staff from the camp started dividing us into groups. My brother and I were registered in Section 8, group 21, on January 8, 1980. We would receive a daily ration of rice, fish, and water.

While I was looking for Section 8, I heard people talking about how their relatives abroad had sent them money and sponsored them to go to another country. They showed each other pictures of their relatives and talked about how they lived in the new country. But I had no relatives abroad.

I found Section 8 at the other end of the camp, far away from the entrance. The group leader distributed a container to carry water, bags of rice, sardines, and a cooking pot to each family. Our group had about twenty families staying under a blue plastic shelter. My brother and I got about five square yards of space. The other families had relatives or friends to help them make a bamboo bed. I had no one to help. Other people in my group did not want to make friends with me because I did not have any gold to show off.

The first night, we slept on the wet ground on a small mat. We were so tired that we slept through the night even as food and other items were smuggled into the camp. The next day, I wrote a letter to David James, who worked for CARE in Bangkok.

That afternoon, my brother and I decided to make a bamboo bed. I had never done this before, but Ra encouraged me to try. First, we dug four holes in the shape of square. We needed four bamboo legs to hold the bed, as well as many pieces of bamboo for the bed slats. With a small knife, we cut bamboo all day. At the end of the day, our legs, hands, and fingers were crossed with bamboo cuts. But we were so proud of our new bed. It felt great to sleep on the bed that night. At midnight, a strong wind blew up and the rain poured hard. We did not much care until we heard our new bed wince slowly like an earthquake and it suddenly dropped us onto the wet, muddy ground. We woke up, chuckled, and realized that we had not dug the holes deep enough to hold the four legs. The next day, I started looking for a job, moving from one section to another, from one agency to another, from the hospital to the sanitation area. Most jobs were filled, but I would not give up hope. I also inquired about my friend Michael Inghim at the Red Cross and other agencies with American volunteers. But no one had heard of him. A week passed quickly.

ᴄᴡ

At night, it was hard to sleep because of the noise and activity as food was smuggled into the camp. Thai soldiers chased the smugglers, arrested them, and beat them up. A woman was raped in the back room near the kitchen by one man after another until she was unconscious. I was shaking and feared for my safety. I stayed aware of people around me.

❧

One afternoon, a man came to my door and asked for me. He told me that an American from Bangkok was looking for me. I was so excited and anxious. I was sure that it was Michael. I told Ra to stay and take care of our belongings.

I followed the man to CARE Section 8 and found David James, whom I'd met at Nong Samith. He told me that he'd received my letter. After a long conversation, he said, "You're safe now. You mentioned in Nong Sameth that you want to work."

"Yes!" I answered.

"I suggest that you go see Mr. Kassie Nou in CARE Section 2. He will have a job for you."

I thanked him and went home, full of joy. Now I had a life to live. God would not close the door on me. When I got home, my brother was waiting for me at the front door. I told him about David and my new job. "You won't have to worry. . . . You can stay home and cook and I'll work," I explained happily. But my joy suddenly turned to sadness. I had no clothes to wear to work. I looked at my only pants, which I was wearing. They were ragged, dirty, and old. They had grown shorter during the long journey. My blouse was full of holes and patched with different colors of cloth. Only my old kramar covered the blouse enough to keep people from looking at my body. I had no sandals to wear. I had to go to CARE the next day. I worried that they would not offer me the job.

Many refugees still traveled back and forth to Nong Samith Camp to see their families or bring them to Khoa I Dang. That evening, my girlfriend from Nong Samith Camp asked me to stay overnight. I decided to borrow her clothes to go to work. "OK, but you have to give me five cans of sardines," she said.

"So you're renting me your clothes?" I asked, surprised. I thought she would let me borrow them. "Five cans of sardines is all I have," I said. "If you take them, I'll have nothing to eat."

"You have a job now, right?" she said. "And you'll get paid!"

I was very excited about my job. I wanted to show myself that I could work and support myself. I wanted to work hard to prove that I was capable of using my brain and my two hands. Why didn't people in my village see me in that way? They thought that all I could do to take care of myself was to sell my body as a prostitute. I woke up early in the morning prepared to go to work. I went to see Mr. Kassie Nou, director of CARE for the Khoa I Dang Camp.

"I can give you a job as an interpreter," he said.

"An interpreter—I do not speak English," I answered.

"You can communicate with David James in English. I think you can do the job," he assured me. He gave me a brief summary of CARE's role and responsibilities in the camp. The organization provided food for lactating mothers and children under five years old. Each camp section had an American volunteer who worked closely with a Cambodian interpreter to serve the mothers and children. There was also a clinic for prenatal care.

Mr. Kassie introduced me to his staff. He gestured toward a man who was sitting at a long bamboo table reading an English newspaper, the *Bangkok Post*. I was very impressed that he could read a newspaper in English. The man dropped the paper in his lap when he heard Mr. Kassie introducing him to me: "This is Sotheary Duong, who was my student in Phnom Penh. He's the interpreter for Section 4."

The man stood up to greet us. He was young, in his early twenties, and very handsome.

"*Chum reap sour,*" I said, which meant "hello" in the Cambodian language. He put both his hands together and smiled before he said hello back. He was dressed in nice new pants and a white long-sleeved shirt tucked into his pants. After we said hello, Mr. Kassie brought me to meet another worker.

I was assigned to work in the prenatal care clinic as an interpreter for Section 2, along with Mr. Duong and two Franciscan nuns from the United States. My salary as an interpreter was three cans of sardines and two cans of sweetened milk per day. As I left the office, I saw my former high school classmate, Sithoeun, who worked at the CARE warehouse. He was married and had a baby girl.

Although I was very happy about my new job, my living situation was terrifying. Shootings, robberies, and smuggling happened every night. Criminals hid out in my shelter. Rapes occurred repeatedly. At night I could not sleep. I heard the cries of rape victims constantly. I had a nightmare every time I closed my eyes. I was depressed but had no one to talk to about it. Sometimes I sneaked sleep at my office at CARE. I was joined there by my co-workers Soeum and Montha. The office became a shelter for us, protected by a security guard at night. We felt safe there.

A month later, I met a man named Heng at the rehabilitation center, where I helped my coworker, Ny, a widow whose husband had been killed during the Communist regime, do rehabilitation for her knee. I thought that Ny and Heng would be a perfect match. He stopped by our office almost every day. Sometimes he brought food and other things for my brother. He also took Ra along to learn English and stayed overnight with him. Since I did not have enough money for my brother to go to the private English class, I agreed to let him go with Heng.

Heng often invited me to have lunch with his sister's family. I refused. I tried to protect my reputation by following the code of conduct that my mother had taught me. In addition, I was poor and I did not want people to look down on me or judge me because of the way I looked or dressed.

A couple of months later, I found out through my brother that Heng was in love with me. He kept sending me letters through my brother, but Ra threw away the letters. Finally, Heng handed me a letter on his own. I rejected his proposal by letting him know that my goal was to get out of the camp first and raise a family later. I told him that I wanted him to be my friend, nothing more. He was brokenhearted but would not give up hope. He came to visit me as usual and tried to persuade me to marry him because he had relatives in the United States. I told him that I wanted to be on my own. I did not want to depend on him and lock myself into being his wife.

After I told him my decision, Heng went completely crazy. He asked me what I didn't like him about him. I told him I didn't like it that he smoked. A week later, he quit smoking. And he asked me to marry him again. I warned him that if he kept proposing to me, I would not consider him a friend anymore.

I felt safer now with the help of police who guarded the camp at night. A couple of months later, CARE managed to raise my salary from sardines to three hundred bath (Thai money, equivalent to about $15) as well as additional dry food and material to make clothes. I felt a lot better.

One rainy day, the Mother Child Health Clinic was leaking, and all my clothes and other things got wet. That night, I laid out the pictures that I had carried from Cambodia to dry on the table in the office. A police officer, Vichet, found the pictures on the table and he loudly questioned, "Whose pictures are these?" "Mine," I responded in a panic. He held up a picture that showed my father and his parents when he was about twenty years old. "This is my great-uncle and aunt," Vichet said, pointing to my grandparents. "They're my grandparents." I said. "And this is my father."

"Oh, my beautiful niece! I held you when you were a baby." He tried to hug me, but I pushed him away.

"No, don't do that. I don't know you," I said. I did not trust him.

"I am your uncle. Your father and I are cousins and we were best friends when we were young," he explained.

We talked on and on about my family and his family until midnight. After that, he came to guard my office and had supper with me and my co-workers every night. I was happy to know that I had a relative on my father's side who was still alive. Vichet brought me to a big shelter near the Section 2 office. He introduced me to my great-aunt and uncle and his own adult children. I met a lot of relatives. They welcomed me and were happy to know that I was alive.

Out of nowhere, a depressed-looking man whom my great-aunt described as brokenhearted stood in front of me. He wore shaggy clothes and his sad face had wrinkle lines and red eyes that showed he did not get enough sleep. He was shocked to see me at his house.

"What's going on here?" he asked.

"This is your niece." My great-aunt made the introduction.

He turned to my great-aunt. "That's her, sister, the one I talked about. Now she is my niece. That's great! Great!" His depressed face faded away, replaced by an overjoyed smile.

"I invited you many times to see my family, but you always refused," Heng said. You are such a good girl." He put his hand on my head.

"Ah, uncle, you behave!" I warned him.

Everyone laughed about the coincidence that a man fell in love with a woman who turned out to be his niece. After that, Heng was never afraid to come visit me. He no longer cared what I said to him. A week later, my great-aunt asked me to become engaged to him. I told them, "I don't want to marry any of my relatives and Heng is my uncle."

"Even when I wasn't your uncle, you never loved me," Heng said.

Not very long after that, my friend Soeum told me that a woman had come looking for me to attack me. She claimed that her husband had had an affair with me. He came to see me at the office every night. After hearing this bad news, I went to see the leader of Section 2 for protection. It turned out that the woman was my uncle Vichet's girlfriend. After that I told my uncle not to come to my office again.

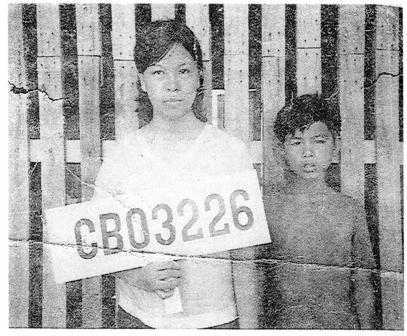

Darina and her brother Chinnara in the Chon Buri processing camp, October 1980

CHAPTER 20

Processing

In August 1980, I saw that the United States and Canada had posted the names of Cambodian refugees who had immediate family members, such as a husband, wife, mother, or father, in those countries. My brother and I looked at the list. Our name was not on it. Of course not—we did not have any relatives living abroad.

That month, for the first time I saw smiles on refugees' faces. The smile of hope for their family's future, especially the children. That was what they lived for—the joy of reunion with family after being separated for so long. They threw away their old clothes and other things. They kept only some clothes and a few pots and pans to use while waiting for processing to leave the camp. They said good-bye to relatives and friends and to this camp where they had lived for months. They were glad to leave this hell with its robbery, abuse, rape, and filth.

My brother woke me up in the morning to see the parade of refugees marching toward their new life. He was happy to see that it was possible to make it to another country. But later, his face turned sad when he asked me, "Sister, when is it our turn?" It was heartbreaking. I told him, "One day!" and smiled to give him hope.

I tried to figure out a way to go to the United States or another country. One of my coworkers felt sorry for me and tried to arrange for me to marry her nephew, who lived in France. My next-door neighbor asked his friend in Texas to sponsor me as his fiancée. One of my neighbors had a brother in Oregon who would also sponsor me as a fiancée. My uncle Heng asked me if I wanted to put my name on the affidavit as his wife to go the United States. I refused.

I really wanted to go to the United States, but I did not want to go as someone's wife. I wanted the freedom to choose a husband who would meet my standards: no drinking, no smoking, more educated than me. . . . So far none of these men fit all my criteria.

When the second list was posted, I felt desperate to find a way out. I thought I could go as someone's wife as a last resort. A couple of weeks later, I received three affidavits of sponsorship. One was from the man in France, another from the man in Oregon, and the third from Texas. The sponsors also sent some money to help me with daily life in the camp.

One day at my office, a middle-aged man came to pick up milk for his baby, and we struck up a conversation. He came from the same province as me. He worked for the American Special Forces, he said, and his family had a sponsor to go to the United States. He encouraged me to send a letter to the U.S. Embassy telling them that I was a former embassy employee. I had never thought about that. He even gave me a sample letter and paid for the postage.

In the meantime, we continued living in the half-empty camp. The place was quieter now, but still scary. In October, a month after I sent a letter to the U.S. Embassy, my brother ran up to me and hugged me. "Sister! Sister!"

"What's up?" I screamed.

"We have . . . . our name . . . our name is on the list," he said, out of breath. He jumped up and danced back and forth. I had never seen Ra so happy. I went to see this posting for myself. Yes, my name was on the list. I was proud of myself. We would make it to another country, as I had planned a year ago. My brother would have a chance for a better future. My parents would not blame me for running away from my village and my other siblings. Their souls would understand the sacrifice I had made and trust me.

As I stood there feeling excited and worried, I heard my friends Montha and Soeum crying inside the office. Their names were not posted yet. Before leaving, I asked my friend Sithoeun and his wife to let Soeum stay with them. Montha would move in with her sister.On October 15, 1980, it was time to say good-bye to my friends Soeum, Montha, Sithoeun, and his family. We cried because we did not know when we would see each other again.

After long hours traveling by bus, Ra and I arrived at the processing camp in Chon Buri at about 2:00 P.M. Chon Buri was a nice, clean camp. The shelters were wood buildings with cement floors, and there were proper bathrooms with good sanitation. Each building was divided into three rooms. We were assigned to a building that we shared with a Chinese family whose case had been deferred by the Canadian embassy. Sotheary, my coworker from Camp Khoa I Dang, was here too. He had been rejected by the Canadian Embassy because he did not have immediate family in Canada. He was working with the Joint Voluntary Agency as an interpreter.

The next day, many refugees departed for the United States, Australia, Canada, France, New Zealand, and other European countries. Some families were sent to a camp in the Philippines to learn how to live in the United States before going there. Other families were rejected by the immigration officers. They stayed and waited for their relatives to do more paperwork.

Soon my brother and I were called for prescreening. A JVA worker asked me if I had any relatives in the States. I told him that I had no one. The United States government had posted my name as a former employee of the United States. The worker explained that this was a special case and required more information. My case was deferred for at least a couple months.

While I waited, I looked for a job to support my brother and me. Ra stayed home to take care of the chores, cook rice, and collect water and charcoal. We felt safe and lived more happily than before. But I worried about the delay in the processing of our documents.

Sotheary, whom I called Terry, told me about a job as a translator for the JVA. I applied and got the job. I worked as part of a team with three other interpreters, including Terry. In my free time, I wrote letters encouraging my friends Sithoeun, Soeum, and Montha to write to the United States Embassy to request political asylum.

Working for the JVA, I did not earn enough money to support my family. I went to look for a friend of my former supervisor in Khoa I Dang who worked for Catholic Relief Services. This woman offered me a job in the transit center distributing food and milk to children and lactating mothers.

In November, I received a letter from an official in the U.S. State Department informing me that under the Privacy Act, he could not disclose Michael Inghim's address to me.

In March 1981, a document about my employment with the U.S. Embassy arrived. I was called to another interview with the Immigration and Naturalization Service. I was accepted by the United States! Finally, I had reached my goal. I would bring my brother to America to escape torture, executions, and unlawful barbarians. I could close my eyes when I died because I knew my brother would be safe and he could have a good future. A day before I left the camp, I received a letter from my sister Dasina saying that she'd arrived safely in Khoa I Dang camp and was staying with a friend. I was worried about her. But I couldn't wait—I had to help myself first. I sent her a letter with the address of my sponsor in New York.

May 15, 1981, was the day I left Thailand for New York City. Before stepping into the plane, I looked back for a last glance of Cambodia in my imagination, to say good-bye. It was night. The cloak of darkness made it difficult to see my last image of the country. But my heart was there.

CHAPTER 21

New York

A GIANT TWA JET TRANSPORTED ME and the other refugees to Oakland, California. We got off the plane and took a bus to an office where our paperwork would be processed. One by one, family by family, we went our separate ways.

Goodbye everyone! I wish you luck in the promised land.

An agent from an organization for refugees helped me and Ra find our way to a plane that would take us to JFK Airport in New York. This plane carried a full load of American passengers, not Cambodians. As we approached the city to land, I saw beautiful lights like the festival of floating lights on the water at home. The tall dark buildings and high bridges looked like dikes in the rice fields in my village. The city looked exactly like the dream I'd had in Bosknor.

I was very anxious to meet my sponsor. I expected an American man or woman to pick us up and drive us home. I left the plane, dragging my brother along and carrying a bag with all my documents. I waited for my sponsor and tried to take care of Ra. He had a high fever and was vomiting.

Two Cambodian men showed up, and one asked, "Are you Darina Siv?"

"Yes," I answered. He asked me to follow him to get my luggage. I went with him, still very curious about my American sponsors. I thought they would be waiting for me in the car. But, after getting my luggage, the four of us took a bus and then went to a subway station.

"The subway is so dirty," I thought. In high school, I had learned that New York was the biggest city in the world. I was so impressed to come to New York. Now, sitting in the subway train, I saw all kinds of marks and drawings that I could not read or understand. The floor was full of trash—empty cans, bags, napkins, and newspapers. I did not ask any questions, though; I pretended everything was fine.

When we got out of the subway, I saw a tall African man wearing ragged clothes. His hands were very dirty. He pulled his cigarette out of his mouth and walked toward me. I could smell alcohol while he talked to me but I could not understand what he said. The younger Cambodian man told me to stay away from him.

We finally arrived at the young man's apartment, on 138th Avenue in Brooklyn. He shared the apartment with his sister and three younger siblings. So we now had a total of seven people in a one-bedroom apartment. My brother and I slept on the floor. There was no difference between a refugee camp and an apartment in New York City.

This young man was Terry's brother, and the HIAS agency had asked him to pick us up from the airport. He told me that Terry and his parents would arrive next month.

For the first couple of days in New York, my brother became more and more sick. His temperature remained high. I was afraid of losing him. But I kept giving him Tylenol until he felt better.

A week later, I went to the social welfare office and enrolled Ra in public school. The people there also gave me some money and helped me find work at an optical company in Manhattan. The job paid $3.35 an hour. My responsibility was to clean glasses. It wasn't hard, but I had to do it fast, on time, and perfectly, and my supervisor kept reminding me of my next assignment. I had two ten-minute breaks and a half-hour lunch. Almost every day, I ran to catch the subway and got lost. I earned $90 to $95 a week.

This was New York, the biggest city in the world, full of people who never smiled or said hello. Every morning, people rushed against time. They read a newspaper with one hand while standing in the train. With the other hand they held their briefcase and ate breakfast. Our neighbors were all strangers. At night we heard an ambulance siren almost every half hour. Guns were shooting off all over the place. I did not like living in New York.

∾

I received letters from friends who had also recently arrived in the states. Sithoeun and his family lived with his uncle in St. Paul, Minnesota. Another friend lived in Florida. She told me about a Catholic sister who had worked with me in the camp and wanted to sponsor me to come to Florida. I wrote her back and expressed my interest in living there.

Terry and his family arrived on June 15. It was a big family reunion. Now we had fourteen people in the one-bedroom apartment. Terry's cousin Theiy, who had lived in New York for five years, offered to let me and my brother stay at her house.

Theiy liked me a lot. She appreciated my good manners. She thought I would make a good wife for Terry.

Terry was a gentleman—kind, open, reasonable, and willing to listen. He fit all three criteria for the man I wanted to marry: he didn't smoke or drink and he was more educated than me. He also believed in God. That was a plus. One thing I did not like about him was that he had a big family. In the Cambodian culture, when I got married, I married my husband's whole family.

After weighing the pros and cons, I decided to marry Terry. I gave my word to Theiy. Terry's family also agreed. They planned the marriage for August 1. Theiy told me not to expect a wedding ceremony like we had in Cambodia. In New York we did not dress up in the traditional wedding costumes.

∽

A month later, Theiy and her husband invited me and Terry to a meeting at the Cambodian Embassy in New York. I dressed up in traditional Cambodian clothing, a pink blouse and a long silk skirt, which I made in Chon Buri camp before coming to the States. Terry wore a suit. Another newly-arrived Cambodian family joined us. We went to a beautiful building near the United Nations headquarters.

It was a high-security building with a metal detector. The elevator brought us up to a beautiful apartment surrounded by windows. The sofas in the living room were precious. The floor was clean and shining. "How wonderful to live in a nice place like this," I thought. While I stood like a statue thinking about this, a tall, handsome man in his late thirties came to welcome us. "Oh God! Is it him? Yes—it's him." As everyone sat down on the beautiful sofas, I was in a state of confusion. My eyes followed the man. But if it was him, why didn't he recognize me? Maybe my appearance had changed so much that he didn't recognize me. I tried to calm down and tell myself that it was not him. The man I suspected looked exactly like Tep Sung Vuth, my first love from high school.

After some socializing, the meeting took place in the conference room, which was surrounded by mirrors. About twenty people were at the meeting. There were two men from Canada, who were Terry's classmates from high school. To my left was a chubby man in his mid-fifties, with Chinese features, light skin, and small, clever eyes. He smiled most of the time. He introduced himself as Eang Sary. This name was all too familiar. In shock, I opened my eyes wide and felt my face and ears flush. I could hardly believe I was meeting him in person—Eang Sary, a high-ranking Khmer Rouge official. I had worked so hard to escape the Khmer Rouge and now I was eating supper with one of their leaders. I noticed that he still wore the black clothes and Ho Chi Minh sandals.

After the meeting, it was time for dinner. The table was full of delicious food like deep-fried shrimp. Under the Communist regime, thousands of people starved to death. But at the Cambodian Embassy, the leaders enjoyed plenty of good food. Did these men know how Cambodian civilians struggled with hunger? In spite of the wonderful food, I was afraid to be around these people.

I talked to the man whom I thought was Tep Sung Vuth. Actually, he was Vuth's brother. His name was Tep Khunnal. I asked him about Vuth. He didn't know anything about him. I was not surprised.

The evening brought back traumatic memories, which gave me nightmares later. I saw the Khmer Rouge soldiers pointing guns at me. I ran away, but then I stepped on a mine, which exploded very loudly. I screamed for help. I woke up short of breath, my body trembling. It took me a couple of hours to fall back to sleep.

The next day, I went to work exhausted because I had not gotten enough sleep. I could not shake the feeling that someone was following me or watching me. At night I was afraid to go to sleep because of the nightmares.

A couple of days later, I sent a letter to my friend in Florida agreeing to be sponsored to go there. I shared my plan with Terry. I asked if he wanted to go with me. He looked puzzled. "Can you wait until August 1?"

"No, I have to go. But you can make your own choice. You can stay with your family. You don't have to go with me," I said. I thought that if this marriage was not going to work out, it should not go any farther.

"You will be my wife," he said. "I must go with you." When I called my sponsor in Florida, she was kind of upset that I was bringing Terry with me, but said she would buy a ticket for the three of us anyway.

With blessings from our elders, Terry and I became husband and wife. Then, on July 15, 1981, we left New York to an uncertain new life in Florida. My transitory life continued as I drifted and searched for a place to settle. I always thought that my arrival in America would be the end of the story. Now I found that it was just the beginning.

CHAPTER 22

Florida

TERRY, RA, AND I ARRIVED at the Orlando Airport around 1:30 P.M. We were met by my sponsor, Adeline. She was seventy-three years old, a retired nurse and a strict Catholic. It took almost two hours to get to her house in a small town called Tavares. It had one grocery store, a couple of gas stations, a post office, and a hospital. Adeline lived in a big house by herself. Her son was a lawyer in Miami.

The house was peaceful, surrounded by trees in a large lot. Many crows and pigeons flew overhead, and brown squirrels jumped from one tree branch to another. The weather made me feel like I was back home in Cambodia. The house had two bedrooms in the front and another that was in a recent addition to the old house. It was very neat and clean. Adeline gave me and Terry the front bedroom, and my brother slept in the living room. Her bedroom was in the new addition.

Adeline kept two turtles in a cage by her bedroom and had a pet cat. The cat had long hair and was mean. She scratched all three of us and bothered Ra at night. He couldn't sleep until he crawled into my bedroom and locked the door. Adeline took very good care of her cat. She shampooed her daily and blew-dry her hair.

There were many rules around the house. Saturday was cleaning day. Terry was in charge of the cleaning. My brother's chore was to take out the trash. I was in charge of vacuuming, cleaning the kitchen, and doing laundry. In addition, Terry and Ra helped cut trees and do yardwork. She also wanted them to clean out the well, which had been built during World War II.

Adeline was busy finding resources for us. She arranged for me and Terry to attend an ESL class. Since it was about an hour's drive from Tavares, she paid a teacher who worked at the school to pick us up.

The first week in Florida, I felt so lonely. There were no Asians around. We had not eaten rice for a week and wondered when we would get some rice. In the morning, we ate cereal and milk for breakfast. We had never had cereal before, but we had to eat what Adeline gave us. At lunch, we ate sandwiches. Since we were used to rice as our main staple, the three of us finished a whole loaf of bread and were still hungry.

The second week, Adeline started complaining that the three of us ate like pigs. One night, my brother crawled into my bed and told me that he was hungry. I sneaked into the kitchen and brought some bananas, apples, and pears for us to eat. We finally fell asleep at 4:00 A.M. The next morning, Adeline called us to see her in the kitchen. We thought she was mad because we had slept late. Instead, she asked us what happened to the fruit in the basket. She said she was reserving that fruit for breakfast. I told her I was sorry, but we were so hungry. She was mad at me. But she liked Ra. She said he was a good boy.

She asked me about my life in Cambodia. I told her about my life when I was young and how I lost both parents and two brothers during the Communist regime. The only thing she had to say was, "I'm sorry that I don't have a maid to serve you."

We continued to feel hungry all the time. Terry and I would walk to the grocery store when Adeline took my brother out someplace. We bought some of each type of fruit to try them. Terry liked apples and I liked cherries. We bought a couple pounds of those and kept them under our bed to eat at night. We were very careful to throw away the trash.

One evening, Adeline told Terry and me that she wanted us to start working and get our own apartment. In addition, she thought she should bring us to apply for food stamps. I agreed to go to work, but Terry wanted to continue going to school. She looked unhappy. After Terry left, Adeline told me that Terry was not a good husband. She thought he was lazy. At his age, he should know how to drive a car . . . etc. She shared with me that she had gotten divorced because her husband had had an affair with her best friend. She believed that all men were bad. They were irresponsible and wanted to take advantage of women. I should divorce Terry.

I was depressed and afraid to tell Terry what Adeline had said. One day, we walked to a mall where Adeline had taken us the previous week. I was good with directions, and if I went someplace one time, I could find it again. When we got to the mall, everyone looked at us. It seemed that the people in this town had never seen Asians before.

As we wandered around the mall, a nice, middle-aged couple sat down and talked with us. I told them about the difficult time I was having. They wanted to help us. After a long talk, they dropped us at home, where Adeline was waiting for us at the front door. She looked angry when she saw the strangers.

Adeline told my brother that Terry and I were bad people. I felt sad and worried. Adeline was looking for an apartment for us, but I had not found a job yet. I understood why she wanted us to leave. I knew it was difficult for her as an elderly lady to take care of the three of us. She did not have enough money. I was willing to work at any job but I did not have any skills.

The next day, Adeline received food stamps worth about $280 for my family. She brought me to the grocery store. Terry and Ra made a long list of what they wanted me to buy for them. They stayed home and cleaned the house.

Adeline pulled one cart and I took another one. She told me to choose my own groceries. After being hungry for two weeks, I eagerly picked out whatever I wanted to eat—many meats, vegetables, and fruits. At the checkout lane, I put all the items on the counter. Suddenly, Adeline grabbed several items and put them in the cart and told me to put them back. At first I thought that $280 in food stamps was not enough to pay for the food. I felt ashamed, looking at her with tears falling down my cheeks while the cashier tried to figure out what was going on. Adeline told the cashier to wait for me until I took the items back.

While driving back home, she accused me of wasting money and buying unnecessary food. I should learn to save money, she said. She kept repeating that she was sorry she did not have a maid to serve me. I told her that I did not need a maid. I could do everything by myself. After that I did not say a word. I cried from the grocery store until we reached her driveway.

As soon as they saw the car, Terry and Ra rushed toward me to get their food. Instead, I walked out of the car crying and went to my bedroom, leaving them to carry in the grocery bags. At supper, only Terry and Ra showed up at the table. I did not want to eat. Adeline asked my brother to get me to come out for supper. She watched me eat like I was a toddler.

That night, my friend Sithoeun called me for the first time. I was so happy to hear his voice because I had not talked in the Khmer language for three months. I told him that if possible I would like to move in with him. Our conversation was interrupted by Adeline. She told me it cost money to talk on the phone long distance.

The next week, the problems escalated. The couple I had met at the mall came to talk with Adeline. They told her they were willing to help us find jobs and housing. Adeline was upset that I had a connection with outsiders.

In my stress and depression, I lost weight and felt sick all the time. My period was also late this month. Terry thought that I might be pregnant. We made a list of the advantages and disadvantages of having a baby. We loved children. But it was not the right time for us to raise a child. We decided to turn to Adeline for help. We told her honestly that we did not want a baby at this time. We were thinking about an abortion. Boom! As soon as Terry spoke this word, she fired back, "I don't want a murderer in my house!" She called my sponsor in New York and said, "I'm sending this young couple back to New York." Next she called the Greyhound bus company and bought three tickets to New York. I begged her to send us to Minnesota, where my friend Sithoeun lived. She refused.

The three of us said nothing. We looked at each other and packed our belongings. That night, Adeline told me she was sorry that things had not worked out well for me. She said, "I spent a total of $645.89 for you, including the airplane tickets from New York and the bus tickets back to New York." I had been in America for three months and I had a debt of $645.89. "You have a choice," she continued. "Either you pay me back, or, if you follow one condition, you won't have to pay me back." I looked at the tablecloth, which was a crochet pattern as complicated as my unresolved problems. "You can donate the money to children in an orphanage so they won't be in trouble like you." I nodded slowly. I continued to pack as she left to go to bed.

On August 8, 1981, Adeline brought the three of us and our luggage to the Greyhound station. While waiting for the bus, she advised me to pick a better person to be my husband. Then she pointed to the picture of the greyhound and said, "You look just like that greyhound." I did not know what she meant. I tried to calm down and said nothing.

Before we left, Adeline told Ra, "You're welcome to come back to visit me, but not your sister." We waved good-bye to her as the bus blew exhaust high into the sky and rumbled out of the station.

∾

It took us two days and nights to reach New Jersey. We had only crumbs of bread to eat. We didn't know how to buy food from the vending machines, and we were afraid to get off the bus. We slept and went to the bathroom on the bus. We got to the New Jersey station around 9:45 P.M. The bus driver told us to get off the bus. We looked around for anyone we knew. No one was around. We were stuck, with no way to get to New York.

We sat down, feeling hopeless. Suddenly, the microphone announced that all passengers traveling to St. Paul, Minnesota, should come to the counter for departure at 11:00 P.M. The word *Minnesota* was familiar to me. I asked Terry to go to the counter. I was shy and afraid to ask. Finally, I got up my courage to talk to the person at the counter. But he did not understand the way I pronounced "Minnesota," without the correct accent. I showed him the address of my friend Sithoeun. He nodded and said, "Yes, that's where this bus is going." I asked, "How much cost the ticket for two big persons and one small person?" "$110 for adults and $65 for a kid," he answered. "Stop!" I said to the cashier, instead of "Wait." I ran to Terry and Ra, and we counted all the money that I had saved in New York. It added up to enough to buy tickets to Minnesota. But when we brought the money to the cashier, there were only two seats left. We begged him to let my brother sit on my lap. Luckily, another passenger canceled her ticket.

Finally, we paid for three tickets. We waited impatiently for eleven o'clock to come. Then we boarded a Greyhound bus bound for Minneapolis/St. Paul.

CHAPTER 23

Minnesota

THE TRIP FROM NEW JERSEY TO ST. PAUL took another two days. We learned how to use the vending machines and discovered that we liked Doritos. We arrived in St. Paul in the morning of August 18, 1981. We hadn't told Sithoeun we were coming, so we took a cab to his apartment on University Avenue.

Sithoeun and his family were surprised to see us. They lived with my friend Soeum in a one-bedroom apartment. I was so happy to see everyone. Soeum and Sithoeun's wife, Sinoy, made us a good lunch. We ate together and had a lot of fun talking all day long. Because the apartment was already crowded, Sithoeun brought us to stay at a friend's house nearby. Sithoeun's uncle, who was president of the Cambodian Association of Minnesota, took me to apply for an AFDC grant.

After qualifying for the grant, I had enough money to rent a one-bedroom apartment on Selby Avenue. We were happy to have our own place, even though it was full of roaches. All three of us slept on the floor because we didn't have enough money to buy a mattress.

∾

Terry and I planned to attend St. Paul Technical College to gain skills that would help us find a job. One evening, we went there to take an entrance test. We thought we would be taking the same test. But we were separated to take different tests. Mine took about two hours. When I left the building, it was very dark out-side. All the window and doors were closed. No one was around. In a panic, I looked for Terry, but he wasn't there. I began to walk home. At the corner of Dale Street and Selby Avenue, in front of an old bar, a giant African American man looked at me. Behind him were three women. I kept walking on the sidewalk as the giant man reached his long arms toward me. I hoped that if I did not bother them, they would not bother me. "Come on, baby! Come on," the man said. The three women clapped their hands and repeated what he said. The man followed me. "Open the door!" he yelled, pointing to his friend, who was sitting in the driver's seat of a car. The closer the man came to me, the more scared I felt. His long arms got closer and closer until they encir-cled me. I was trapped. Finally, I sneaked out under his left armpit and ran, tripping on my high heels. I pulled off the shoes and ran home with bare feet.

I made it to our apartment, but Terry was not there. I was afraid to be alone. My body was shaking, and my breath came out fast. An hour later, Terry came with Sithoeun and a couple of friends. When he couldn't find me at the school, he had walked home. I wasn't there, so he went to Sithoeun's apartment to ask for help finding me.

We had no transportation. Most of time, we walked from place to place. While walking one day, we came upon a garage sale. Ra liked a kid's bike that cost about three dollars. I bought it for him. The small bike was very helpful in carrying our gro-ceries, especially fifty-pound bags of rice and watermelons. But the poor bike broke because it couldn't hold so much weight. Then I learned to take the bus.

I passed the technical college test with high scores. Unfor-tunately, the welfare system would not allow both Terry and me to go to college at the same time. Terry decided to go to the tech-nical college, and I enrolled in an adult education learning cen-ter. My brother attended public school.

While I was preparing to take the GED, my social worker told me that I had to look for job. A human resources representative from an insurance company came to interview students for job openings. She encouraged me to apply for an entry-level job with the company.

In April 1982, I started working at the The St. Paul Companies as a record clerk, for $4.50 an hour. With this income, I would support my family. Terry planned to attend the University of Minnesota, and my brother was entering high school. I was the first Cambodian to work at the insurance company. I worked in the claims department.

During the first six month of my job, my supervisor, JN, never said hello to me. Nonetheless, I liked the job very much and learned it quickly. I arrived on time every day and worked hard without a break. One of the managers of the claims department passed my cubicle every day on his way to get his coffee and always saw me working so hard. He put his thumb up and said, "Good job!" That's how I learned what the thumbs-up gesture meant. I understood English very well when my coworkers asked me to do something, but I couldn't express my thoughts or feelings in English. Mostly I smiled to show I understood. I tried to be friendly to all my coworkers. Everyone seemed to like me, but they imitated my accent. At lunch, I was afraid to go to the cafeteria because people would come up to see what kind of food I had. Some people made jokes or comments, and others made a face. I ate lunch in my cubicle. Someone smelled my food and came in. He said, "I heard that your people eat cats and dogs. I'm worried about my friend who lost his cat recently."

On the bus on my way home from work, people asked me where I came from, whether my country had a currency, and if I had ever seen cars or brick houses. Sometimes people on the street angrily accused me of stealing their jobs. At our apartment, two boys threw rocks at the wall and screamed at us to go home. I thought that this must be how refugees were treated in the

United States. It made me miss my home very much and feel sorry for myself to have to be a refugee.

After two months on the job, I had learned everything and usually completed my work by around 2:00 P.M. I went to my supervisor and asked for more things to do. My coworkers said, "You're crazy." My supervisor told me to go and help the clerks with the property and liability files. I could find lost files in an hour while it took my coworkers all day. Everyone gave me their work to do while they took a break. By the end of six months, I knew the file numbers in three units. I was well known in the department for finding lost files.

My supervisor still didn't say hello to me. She left for maternity leave before my review. The assistant manager, Shirley, gave me my review form. On a scale of 1 to 10, I rated myself, 4, 5, and 6. During the review, Shirley said, "You checked 4, 5, and 6." I smiled. She gave me 8s and 9s and told me that my performance was outstanding. When my supervisor returned from maternity leave, she was much nicer to me. She started to say hello every morning. I learned what "outstanding performance" meant.

When I was looking for lost files by the claim managers' desks, I noticed all the degrees the managers had. I wondered how to get a degree so I could have a job like theirs. I knew I had to go back to school. One manager said to me, "Shouldn't you be in high school, kid?" "No, I'm twenty-five years old and married," I answered and chuckled. "I thought you were just a kid running around my desk," he laughed.

Bored with my job, I applied for positions at the next grade level. Finally I got a level 2 job, as a mail clerk. My supervisor was a very nice lady, fifty-five years old. She hoped that I wouldn't quit the job—she'd lost a couple of workers before me. I worked by myself in the basement supply room with a telephone and a radio. I delivered mail to the home office and dropped mail for the van driver to pick up.

The basement was very dusty, and I developed allergies. In

addition, I had to run every morning to catch the bus. I breathed cold air into my lungs all winter long, and I didn't have adequate winter clothes. I caught colds and the flu quite often. Still, I never called in sick. I was afraid of losing my job, because I was supporting my husband and brother on my income of less than $600 per month. As long as I could walk, I went to work.

In April 1983, I was promoted to data entry clerk. I did coding and entering for new customer applications. I learned the computer in a week. The department was very busy, and our supervisor encouraged everyone to work as much as possible, including Saturdays and Sundays. My overtime added up to thirty hours a week.

∾

In June that year, my sister Dasina arrived from the Philippines, where she'd been in a processing camp after leaving Khoa I Dang. Terry and I also decided to sponsor a girl from a Cambodian orphanage. Now our family had five members. The apartment was too crowded, so we moved to a duplex. Later, Sina asked me to help her friend Thaly and her family of three move to Minnesota from Alabama. I agreed to help them. The nine of us lived together happily, even though space was tight. We saved enough money to buy our first car, a 1980 Oldsmobile. We were glad that not to have to walk or take a city bus except to go to work. Thaly's family found a house, and my family moved again to a house on Como Avenue, near Como Park behind the State Capitol.

In the fall of 1983 I passed my GED test and got my driver's license. I began taking an ESL class in the evenings at a community college. My teacher, Mrs. Matel, encouraged me to take more classes.

I sponsored another relative, Kun, to come to St. Paul. He was about seventeen years old. Sina's friend Sin also came to live with us after her brother moved to California. Now Terry and I lived with five teenagers.

In early 1984, I developed pneumonia four times in a month. Terry begged me to take a break from working overtime. I did not listen to him. I hid my wheezing and my difficulty breathing. I could not sleep at night. One day in March, after working late, I was so tired I fell asleep on Terry's shoulder. When he put his arm around me, I was suddenly awake and felt like I was drowning. I could not breathe, but I tried to pretend I was fine. Terry looked puzzled. I called a doctor and described my symptoms. The doctor asked me to breathe into the phone. He recommended that Terry bring me to the emergency department right away. I was hospitalized for five days with an oxygen tube and IV. I'd had a severe asthma attack.

In the hospital, I could not sleep because I was short of breath. I wanted to sit down, but my body ached. I wanted to walk, but I was so dizzy, I almost fainted. I wished I would die to end this suffering, but the oxygen tube in my nose kept me alive. The medication they gave me made my body shake. I felt like bugs were crawling under my skin. I was hungry even though my belly was full. I had nightmares. I felt like my body had been dropped from the sky. My heart pounding sounded like a grandfather clock. Terry was with me constantly to help me move, go to the bathroom, and eat. He gave me massages for my pain and stayed overnight at the hospital in spite of his many assignments at school. I felt terrible. I swore I would not work overtime again. Why did I need money if my body was full of pain? My deceased parents were unable to bring anything with them or leave anything for their children. Money and property vanished in a second.

After my release from the hospital, I was still weak and unable to work for a couple of days. I was on an inhaler. The doctor ordered me to work only half time for a week. Because of the medication, I gained twenty pounds. I was hungry all the time. After my sickness, I felt I had to work smart, not hard. In the company job postings, I saw more than ten postings for computer programmers, with a salary triple my paycheck. I wanted to become a computer programmer. At the same time, I applied for a rater/coder job, which was level 4. But when I interviewed for the job, the person in human resources told me I needed to take some communication classes.

Sina and Sin graduated and got jobs. They moved out to an apartment of their own. Terry also got a job, as a teacher at Highland Park High School. Terry, Ra, and I moved again, to a big old house.

After unsuccessfully applying for the rater/coder job four times, I gave up. I quit my full-time job to go to school. My goal was to become a computer programmer, even though I didn't know exactly what it involved.

My savings from all my hard work was enough to buy another car for me to drive to school. In the fall of 1984, I became a full-time student at Lakewood Community College, majoring in data processing. I was the only Asian in my computer classes. I used a tape recorder to keep up with the teachers' lectures. If questions on a test came from the textbooks, I always got an A. If the question came from a lecture, I got a C or D.

We were broke most of the time. We budgeted our money to pay for gas and groceries for a week, until the next paycheck came. Ra worked hard as a paper carrier, saving enough money to buy an old car of his own. Even though we did not have money, we were very happy. We had time to go fishing and go to the park, on picnics, and to weddings. In the last five years, I had finally fallen in love with Terry, who was so caring and understanding. He was fun, too.

❧

Although my day-to-day life was improving, the past haunted me every night. I dreamed about soldiers chasing me with guns. I woke up in the middle of the night screaming, sweating, and short of breath. Terry, too, screamed and moved his arms and legs as he slept. When he woke up, he told me that he saw soldiers torturing people, and he was next. We went to work and school exhausted. I felt that someone was following me when I was driving. I heard the voice of the girl screaming "injustice" before the soldiers executed her in Sam San. I was afraid of people who wore black clothes and I afraid to touch black clothing. I was also afraid of the mailman, police officers, and anyone else in uniform. One day, the mailman delivered a certified letter to me. As soon as I opened the door and saw the mailman, I closed it again.

I felt guilty to be alive, because I had left my siblings behind. I cried when I saw the school bus picking up students. I thought about my siblings in Cambodia—my brothers Darinal and Chhinaro, my sisters Sokna and Soknaroeun. They might be suffering with no food. I became angry easily and turned happy just as suddenly. It seemed like there were two people fighting in my head all day long. At night, the nightmares returned. I was afraid to stay by myself. I could not stay in a locked room or a room with no doors or windows. I chastised myself for escaping in 1979. I should have stayed in the Communist zone and let the soldiers kill me, so I would not have to suffer like this. Why had I learned to lie and steal to survive just to suffer like this? I thought of many ways to kill myself, such as a car crash or by running onto the freeway. When I was alone, I cried most of the time. I felt sorry for Terry because I was hard to live with, but he supported and encouraged me to live to keep my hope of helping my family who were left behind.

I looked for a part-time job to block these feelings. I worked as a temp, on call for any job, including janitorial, factory, assembly, clerical, and banking. Terry worried about me because I worked at night. When I got home, he was waiting up for me.

Besides working in a variety of jobs, I liked to go fishing. The place I liked the most was Welch Village in Cannon Falls. A river there flowed liked the river in my village. Along the riverbank were many tall trees. The place scared me at first. It reminded me of a spot in Sam San where the Khmer Rouge executed many innocent people. I could not stay long. But I forced myself to go back. The third or fourth time, more Asian people came. Families cooked corn and fish and had lunch together. The more I went to Welch Village, the more safe I felt among the tall trees and bushes. Sometimes I watched the sun set over the cornfield and remembered the time I waited for my grandfather to come back from his fishing trip. Near the cornfield, there were cows and horses. When people drove by, the dust blew up into the sky. The scene looked liked my village in the evening before sunset.

❧

My body continued to suffer many aches and pains. I had a severe headache every day for three to four hours. I kept taking Tylenol and "coining"—rubbing a quarter on my back along the rib cage—to circulate my blood and. I had no hobbies. I did not like crowds. Sometimes I was weak and exhausted for no reason. I could not watch violent movies. My favorite television show was *Little House on the Prairie*. I went to see a doctor for my asthma, but I thought the symptom might be related to posttraumatic stress.

In 1988, a Khmer monthly newspaper announced a Khmer Festival in Long Beach, California. There would be art, music, a literature contest, and the Miss Cambodia contest. The festival was open to all Khmer people in the United States. I decided to enter the literature contest. But the due date was in just two weeks, and I wondered how I was going to complete my story in so short a time.

In a 5 X 7 notebook, I started to write the story of my life. Every day for more than a week, I went to school, came home and wrote until two or three A.M., got a couple of hours of sleep, then went back to school. Then I had three final exams at the end of the quarter. I completed two of the exams but couldn't finish a take-home exam and some programming for my computer lab class. I decided to take an incomplete in order to finish my story. Terry sat next to me and did his homework and massaged my back. I kept a bottle of Tylenol at hand. Sometimes I fell asleep on the table. When I woke up, I continued to write. I skipped supper some nights. I filled one page after another very fast. I couldn't believe how good my memory was—I felt like I was watching my life on a big movie screen. I finished my story in twelve days. It was a great release, despite my severe pain.

After completing the book, I took a long trip with my brother Ra to Springfield, Illinois, to visit a woman we knew from the camp. Then we visited a great-aunt in Philadelphia and other relatives in Connecticut and New Jersey. We also went to New York for the first time since we'd left there in 1981.

Ra graduated from high school in 1987 and entered St. Cloud State University. I was thirty years old. Terry and I thought it was about time for us to have children. I planned to have my first baby after graduating with my Associate in Applied Science degree the next year.

My first pregnancy was terrible. I had night sickness instead of morning sickness. I attended school every day, but as soon as I got home at around 2:00 P.M., I vomited. I could not eat or drink. I could not tolerate the smell any kind of food, even if it was just coming through Terry's body odor. He had to sleep with my brother. I covered my head with a blanket to protect myself from the smell of food. When I was about three months pregnant, I was driving back from dropping Ra off at the dormitory in St. Cloud when I swerved off the road. I quickly jerked the steering wheel. Luckily, I got back onto the main freeway. Shaking, I drove slowly in the right lane until I got home safely.

I still had nightmares, and sometimes I seemed to halluci-nate as well. One day at noon, while taking a nap, I heard my front door open and footsteps walk in. Then I saw my great-grandfather, who passed away in 1972. He complained about the difficult time he had finding my house. Behind him was my great-aunt, whose family was executed. She brought a couple of her kids with her. My uncle walked behind them. After I let them in, my mother appeared in beautiful pink blouse and a traditional long skirt, the one I dressed her in when she died. In her right arm she carried my baby brother. She hurried in and told me, "They've let me out just for today and I only have a couple hours to visit you." I did not ask them any questions. It seemed I was very busy serving them food and drinks. My house was full of relatives who had passed away. In Ra's bedroom, I found my father and my fourth brother sitting quietly near Ra's bed with sad, tired faces. My father wore short pants and an old gray shirt and held his red and white kramar in his hand. Later, my mother screamed that it was time for her to go back. Then, one by one, my great-grandfather, my great-aunt and her children, and my uncle left through the front door.

The sound of noisy footsteps woke me. I opened my eyes and looked around to see if I was still dreaming. No, I was awake and aware that everyone was gone except my father and my fourth brother. I went quickly to Ra's room to look for them. I found nothing. I sat down on the floor trying to understand what had happened.

The cramps and pain made my pregnancy horrible. At five months, it felt like a sharp needle was drilling inside all my bones. The Tylenol did not help anymore. I went to see the doctor, and he said these feelings were part of pregnancy.

One Friday evening when I was eight months pregnant, Ra came home from St. Cloud for a visit. He parked his car behind my car and went out with a friend. I was in a hurry to get to my evening class at Lakewood Community College. Terry told me to take Ra's car for the evening. As I drove on the freeway, the speedometer indicated that the car was slowing down even though I kept pumping the accelerator. When the speed dropped to 40 miles per hour, I pulled to the side of the road to find out what was wrong. I turned off the engine but did not know what to do.

It was March, and the weather was still chilly, with some snow on the ground. I was cold. I sat in the car for about five minutes until I saw some kind of smoke coming from the engine on the passenger side. I grabbed my backpack, put my coat on, and got out of the car. On the freeway, the traffic was jumping. I leaned against the car as smoke rose higher and higher into the sky. One man stopped and asked if there was something he could do for me. I told him to call my husband at home to let him know that my car had broken down. He left. The cloud of smoke got bigger and bigger. A brown van stopped under the bridge and the driver made a sign for me to walk toward him. His teenage daughter stood near him. "Come on! Come on!" he said slowly. As I got close to him, I heard a sound like a mine explosion. I turned around and saw that Ra's car had exploded. The smoke and flames shot high into the sky. The fire spread toward the front seat.

Soon, the police and a fire crew came to put out the fire. By the time they arrived, flames were burning most of the car. The gentleman who had taken my phone number to call Terry came back and told me that there was no answer. I remembered that Terry always turned off the phone when he took his nap. After his nap, he went to his evening class. A police officer asked me to stay in the back of his car. I felt like a convicted felon. The firefighters sprayed water on the fire, and the police called a tow truck to haul the car away. The police brought me home. Thanks to three strangers, the police, and the firefighters, my life was saved.

I prepared to graduate in the summer of 1988. My baby was due in May. Three weeks before the due date, I heard someone pounding a hammer on my front door. I went downstairs and found a notice that "these premises are unfit for habitation." I called my landlord. He told me I should look for another apartment. I would be homeless if I could not find another apartment.

Two weeks later, we were contacted by a local group that was going to purchase our building and remodel it as part of a neighborhood improvement plan. The woman offered financial support for my family to relocate. We found an apartment and would move in June.

Two weeks later, the baby was born. After a difficult labor of twenty-three hours, the doctor decided to perform a cesarean section. Less than an hour later, I had a baby girl of seven pounds, twelve ounces. As soon as I knew my baby was a girl, I fell into a deep sleep while Terry held and kissed her. We named her Nancy Saathia.

When I got home, I received my final exam in the mail. In June 1988, we moved into the new apartment and I finally graduated. By this time, I no longer wanted to be a computer programmer. It was boring to work with machines. I liked helping people.

In September, I started working as an educational assistant for the St. Paul public schools, but I soon quit to pursue my bachelor's degree at Metro State University, with a double major in computer information systems and human services. I worked at a part-time job at the Khmer Youth Leadership Program while going to school full time.

✦

In 1989, my sister Sina married a man named Bob, and they bought a house on Goodrich Avenue. In April the next year, my family moved into a house across the street from Sina and Bob. On August 25, 1990, Terry and I had our second baby, George Asana. That year I began working full time as a counselor for a program for Southeast Asians. I worked with one client who had terminal cancer. Working with her almost every day gave me flashbacks to my own trauma. But my boss did counseling with me so I would not bring these problems home. For two years, I suffered with my client as she screamed for help. When she died, I was in charge of her funeral.

My posttraumatic stress was getting better and better. The people who argued in my head still bothered me. I was writing another novel to release them onto the page. It was a classic love story about a couple who were engaged before the Communist regime. After the fall of the Khmer Republic regime, the man became a Khmer Rouge soldier while the woman was considered New People. In 1991, I self-published my book.

Publishing that book allowed me to heal. I was able to be "me," a normal person, again. I realized that I had the ability to laugh, to enjoy my family and friends, to find things interesting. I became more involved in the community, helping cook for the Khmer New Year and assisting other people when they needed help. I became a foster parent and cared for Cambodian orphans. I felt like a brand-new person, different from the "I" I had known in the last five years.

CHAPTER 24

Return To Cambodia

THE DREAM OF VISITING MY FAMILY who were left behind in Cambodia was always on my mind. Sina had gone there and brought me pictures, videotapes, letters, and food, which made me even more excited and anxious to go. In my dreams, I went to visit my family, but I never saw them. My dream was not complete. In December 1991, I began planning a trip to Cambodia for the following May. My friend Montha, who lived in Missouri, would join me. Terry offered to take care of the children while I was gone.

At first I was so excited. I planned to do whatever I wanted to do because this was my own country and I was Cambodian. I would visit places I'd never been before in Phnom Penh. I would walk along the beautiful streets to get some fresh air. I would buy food on the sidewalk and enjoy my favorite foods that I hadn't had in more than ten years. Many fruits were on my list, such as delicious jackfruit, crispy green mango, sweet mangustant, honey logan, tasty rambutant, and fresh duran, banana, sweet pineapple, papaya, and coconut. . . . I had daydreams and night dreams of seeing my home, my sisters, brothers, aunts, uncles, villagers, the place where I lived with my family and the place where I suffered hunger. I planned to visit my elementary school and ride a bike to my high school and visit my high school classmates who survived. I would ask them to come and stay overnight with me so we could talk and talk. I would swim in the river. Wow! So much fun . . . for five months I dreamed about all the fun things I would do in Cambodia. I couldn't wait for May to come. I wrote to my uncle John in Phnom Penh, letting him know of my arrival in May.

∾

On May 21, 1992, Montha and I left for Cambodia. Nancy had just turned four years old, and George was twenty-one months. I hugged my children before boarding the Northwest Airlines jet. I was afraid to leave.

The flight from Minneapolis to Bangkok lasted twenty-four hours, with one stop in Japan. There was nothing to do but sleep, eat, and watch movies. I was worried about our safety in Cambodia. We'd heard rumors of bad things happening to travelers. We reached Bangkok at midnight. The next morning, we flew from Bangkok to Phnom Penh, which took about fifty minutes. The airplane was full of a United Nations team coming to help establish peace in Cambodia while elections were being held. We arrived at Pochintong Airport at about 10:45 A.M. It was a very small, quiet airport. Oh! It was so hot, and the sun shone in the open sky. As soon as I got off the plane, I started sweating like I'd taken a shower.

Montha's sister came and picked her up. My aunt Heng stood waiting for me outside the building. She didn't recognize me until I called her name. "Is that you, Rina?" she called. "Don't you recognize me?" I asked. "Oh, God, you're so fat! So beautiful!" she exclaimed. As we drove to John's house, I noticed that the street was crowded with motorcycles and bikes that didn't follow any traffic rules. The street was also very dirty. People threw their water left over from cleaning dishes or clothes into the street. There was no drain to carry the water away.

Our car stopped in front of a long, old building. I got out of the car and stepped in the dirty water. We went up to John's apartment on the second floor. His apartment did not have air conditioning. Steamy hot waves melted my body into a river. I was exhausted from the heat and nauseous with the smell of the dirty water. I almost thought of returning to the United States.

I walked with John to use a phone in a nearby hotel to call Terry and let him know that I had made it to Phnom Penh safely. I was dressed liked other Cambodians, but everyone looked at me and called me names—"American," "Filipino," "John's wife," "immigrant," "foreigner."

"Why don't these people see me as Cambodian?" I asked John. "What's wrong with them?" I felt sad because I was not accepted as a Cambodian. When I tried to explain, people laughed and said that I was trying to be Cambodian.

My aunt was busy cooking for me. I went to the market, where I saw ripe mangos that I wanted to buy. I stood behind a customer who negotiated a price of 4,000 riels for a kilo of mangos. I planned to buy at least ten kilos. But the vendor looked at me and told me the price was 8,000 riels per kilo. I went back to John's apartment without buying anything. I told my aunt what had happened. She laughed. "What's so funny?" I said. "I am Cambodian and my own people reject me." As I talked about my disappointment, Heng continued to laugh. I told myself that this reaction was because the people in Phnom Penh did not know me well.

The next morning, we woke up at 4:00 A.M. and walked to the bus station. My aunt knew a bus driver who lived in the same village in Pursat Province where I used to live. The bus was an old minivan, which I called "Great Grand Van" because it was older than me. There was no key to start the engine. The driver jump-started it by touching two electric wires. As Great Grand Van drove out of Phnom Penh, it was stopped frequently at checkpoints. At each checkpoint, the driver gave money to the soldiers. At some spots, the soldiers pointed guns at the driver and demanded more money, which scared me.

The van got out of Phnom Penh and headed toward Pursat

on National Route 5. At first, I was afraid to look at the rice fields full of palm trees. They reminded me of the killings, torture, and executions. My mind started to spin with bad feelings like a bottle of dirt and water being shaken. I kept my eyes inside the bus and talked to no one. I did not want the other passengers in the bus to realize that I was from America.

The road was terrible. No one had repaired it since the Communist regime. The van traveled thirty-five to forty miles an hour and my head constantly bumped against the roof. We crossed a hole as big as a well full of water and mud, and the back wheels of the van got stuck. The driver drove back and forth but that just dug us in deeper. The driver asked his crew to get out and push the old van. Finally we made it out of the deep mud.

The farther we got from Phnom Penh, the worse Route 5 became. In front of us were many cars and trucks in a line. The bus driver stopped for a minute to observe the situation and then drove out of the line, off the road, and across a rice field. The rice had recently been harvested, which left many bumps all over the place. Incredibly, the Great Grand Van made it through the rice field.

It was about 11:00 A.M. We still had a long way to go. All the passengers except me fell asleep in spite of the bumpy roads. They did not seem worried about the road or any danger. I was full of anxiety, however. The next obstacle was a broken-down old bridge. I volunteered to get out of the bus, but the driver said, "It will be fine!" The Great Grand Van got stuck on two broken pieces of wood in the middle of the bridge. I looked down, wondering why I had come here. Below us was a deep lake full of lotus and yellow water where many buffalo slept. If the van could not make it across the bridge, I would be dead and would leave two small children in the States without a mother. I thought I was out of my mind to have come back to Cambodia. While I was busy stressing out and chastising myself, my Great Grand Van got safely over the bridge.

After many more difficulties on the route, we reached Pursat City around 2:30 P.M. Children were playing in the street. People were working at their homes. The van stopped in front of my grandmother's house. My aunt got out first and I followed her. I stood with a happy smile to greet the people who came and circled me. First I called my grandmother. "Are you really Rina?" she asked. "Yes!" I answered. Everyone cheered and welcomed me—my sister Sokna, my uncle, my aunt, cousins, neighbors. My youngest sister, Soknaroeun, did not recognize me. She was very disturbed, with severe schizophrenia.

That night all my relatives—over thirty people—stayed at my grandmother's small house. I had no proper place to sleep. The mosquitoes bit me all night long.

In the morning, big red mosquito bites covered my face and hands. I asked my brother Chhinaro to bring me to my village, Kompang Rokar. We traveled by motorcycle. I saw that everything had changed in the past twelve years: roads, houses, people. In my village, too, nothing was the same.

As I stood near where my family's house used to be, I tried to recall the good feelings about my home. But they were no longer there for me. The past twenty years had stolen all my good memories. There was nothing left for me except myself. Was I really the same person I had been twenty years ago?

Feeling sad, I went back to Pursat with my brother. I had no words when my relatives asked me what I had seen.

I realized that I had to accept these changes. I could not stay stuck in the past but had to move on to live in the present and plan for the future. I was not seventeen years old anymore, a single girl trapped in a traditional, restrictive culture. I was a married Khmer woman with a family to take care of, and I lived in the United States, not Cambodia.

During my second week in Pursat, I volunteered with CARE and with the United Nations to visit repatriated Khmer people in Bakan, near the Thai border. In Bakan, I asked the refugees about the difficulty of coming back to Cambodia, how long it had taken them to come back, and what things they received from the United Nations. As I did the interviews, children stood by and watched me. They called me an "American who could speak very good Khmer." At first I thought they were teasing me. I explained to them that I was Khmer, but they laughed and said I wanted to be Khmer, just what the people in Phnom Penh had said. The children called their friends to come look at me. About twenty kids circled me, saying, "Hello! Hello!" They repeated this over and over until it got on my nerves because I could not interview people. Out of patience, I screamed at them to shut up. But they continued laughing and making fun of my Khmer pronunciation and saying "That American speaks Khmer very well." It was around noon, and the heat was building. The kids continued to bother me. Finally I yelled at them using a Khmer swear word. They applauded and said they had never heard another American say that word.

When I was done working, I walked toward the United Nations pickup truck. The kids ran after me, still saying, "Hello, hello." I went inside the truck and locked the door. Even young kids were labeling me as an American. "What's wrong with me?" I thought.

I went back home very tired and did not say a word. I missed my children at home. Now I knew I did not belong here. After fifteen years away from my homeland, I could not be called Khmer anymore. In a way, my grandmother was right when she told me I could never come back.

At the end of the third week, I went back to Phnom Penh, anxious to go home. I went shopping with my aunt for some silk to bring home. On the way back to John's house, I saw a crowd of people on the street arguing about something. Suddenly, guns were shooting in my direction. Heng jumped off the bicycle and fled to find shelter. The crowd moved back and forth in confusion. My aunt called from a distance, "Rina! Get off the bike!" I ran toward her. We hurried into John's apartment and closed the door.

∽

Just across the street from John's apartment, on the Mekong River, there was a bar that played very loud music every night. I asked John if we could go there just to see what it looked like. I had never been to a bar either in America or in Cambodia. He refused. He didn't like that bar. The music bothered him so much at night that he had to wear earplugs. When John went to Bangkok one day, I asked his landlady to bring me to the bar. Many girls as young as fourteen or fifteen were dressed up and wore heavy makeup. They stood in two lines waiting to welcome guests. As soon as we walked in, the girls rushed to welcome us, but they were disappointed and backed off from us when they saw that we weren't men. The bar was full of United Nations soldiers, many gray-haired men, and a few young men. I found out that the girls worked as prostitutes at night and went to school during the day. Some of the girls came from rural areas and sent the money they made to their parents back home. Some girls had been kidnapped and were forced to work in the bar because they had no way back to their village.

By my fourth week in Cambodia, I was feeling terrible. I missed my children so much. I made many telephone calls just to hear them talk. One day lasted so long it seemed like a week. On the day of my return to Minnesota, my relatives came with me to the airport. They were all sad. I was happy to go back to see my family.

In June 1992, at the Minneapolis St. Paul airport, my daughter and son were waiting for me. Nancy gave me some beautiful dried flowers that she had saved from Mother's Day. My son gave me a big hug and kisses.

My trip to Cambodia showed me something about my identity. In the past two decades, I had been labeled many names.

Before 1975, I was called a Republican. After 1975, I was one of the New People. When I walked to the Thai border, I was called a hobo and later a refugee. In America, before I became a United States citizen, I was a Cambodian refugee. Now I was a United States citizen, but I did not call myself an American. I am Cambodian, a Cambodian who lives in the United States of America. Even though my Cambodian people rejected me, I still am Cambodian.

After the trip, I valued and appreciated my life more than I had before. I had new hope to live for the future, especially my two children, Nancy and George. The past is just the past—a past that leaves me with painful memories, a past that stays with me so I can tell my children or the next Khmer generation about the unforgettable tragedy of a beautiful country called Cambodia. For my family left behind in that country, I will continue to send money to support them the best I can.

In March 1993, I received an acceptance letter from the University of St. Thomas into the three-year Master of Social Work program. For the next three years, I worked full time, took classes in the evenings and on weekends, and was a mother and housewife. When I got home after my evening classes, my family was already in bed. I rushed to do the family's cooking for the next day and then finished my homework assignments. Sometimes, I woke up early in the morning and found my plate of food on the couch with me and my boots full of melted snow. Every minute was precious. While I did my homework, I also cooked rice, put dirty clothes in the laundry, made phone calls, checked my children's homework, and wrote a list for Terry of things to do the next day.

For three years during graduate school, I lost contact with my friends and family. On a typical day, I drove from place to place for my job and walked from building to building for my classes.

Other students in the program struggled to handle the many classes, the practicum, and the assignments. I had to make my best effort in triple the time of these students because English was not my native language. For my clinical research paper, I wrote about "Spiritual Healing in Cambodian Culture and Mental Health." I asked my grandmother, who was a spirit caller, for help with my paper.

∽

On May 13, 1996, dressed in my black graduation gown, I sat in the front row of the college auditorium waiting for my name to be called. A few tears slid down my cheeks and my heart opened as I bowed my head to comfort myself in my excitement. I remembered the dedication I put on my final paper: "I would like to dedicate this clinical paper to my beloved parents, who taught me the great value of education. You believed that one day, by patience and commitment, I would achieve the goal of Master of Social Work in order to help myself and Cambodian society." I felt that my parents' souls were with me in this room, smiling and proud of me. I had seen them give me this look when I passed the national exam to enter junior high school. I also heard my father's voice whisper into my ear, "I know you can make it."

One by one, more than a hundred graduate students in social work and nursing walked to the podium. My name was called. I heard the applause from the audience and my children cry out, "Mommy!" I smiled as my instructor handed me the folder. I was so glad to have the chance to be a role model for my children.

After the ceremony, my family waited for me outside the building. The twilight fell with a soft gentle wind that blew the tree branches and leaves, sounding like applause for the success of all the graduate students. I walked toward my children, who were enjoying cake and punch. They gave me a big hug, and I gave Terry a beautiful loving smile. "Now it's your turn for your Ph.D., honey!" I said.

About the Author

After coming to the United States as a refugee in 1981, Darina Siv and her husband settled in St. Paul, Minnesota. Darina earned her B.A. in human services and computer information systems in 1992 and a M.S.W. from the University of St. Thomas in 1996. From 1990 to 1999, she worked as a counselor at the Wilder Foundation Social Adjustment Program for Southeast Asians in St. Paul. Most of her work involved counseling Cambodian clients who had post-traumatic stress disorder. In working with them, she used techniques of self-healing.

From 1999 to the present, Darina has worked as Executive Director of the United Cambodian Association of Minnesota, Inc. Her goal and vision is to contribute her social work skills to help her community. She has also volunteered with Cambodian refugees in a number of capacities.

Darina's awards include a Leadership Initiative Neighborhood Program award, a Certificate of Commendation from Governor Rudy Perpich, and the Nou Hach Award for the Long Novel, for a novel she wrote in the Cambodian language.